The Snouters

The Snouters
Form and Life of the Rhinogrades

Harald Stümpke

QUONDAM CURATOR OF THE MUSEUM OF
THE DARWIN INSTITUTE OF HY-YI-YI,
MAIRUWILI

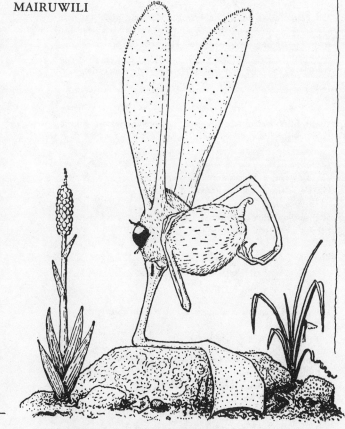

Epilogue by Gerolf Steiner
Translated by Leigh Chadwick

The University of Chicago Press
Chicago and London

This Phoenix edition is published by arrangement with
Doubleday & Co., Inc.

The Snouters was originally published in Germany, under the title *Bau
und Leben der Rhinogradentia,* by Gustav Fischer Verlag Stuttgart in
1957. Copyright © 1964 by Gustav Fischer Verlag Stuttgart.

Portions of the book appeared in *Natural History* magazine in April,
1967 and is reprinted here with permission.

The 15 plates and 12 text figures in this volume were drawn by
Gerolf Steiner.

The University of Chicago Press, Chicago 60637
The University of Chicago Press, Ltd., London

Library of Congress Cataloging in Publication Data
Stümpke, Harald.
    The snouters.

    Translation of: Bau und Leben der Rhinogradentia.
    Bibliography: p. 89
    1. Animals—Anecdotes, facetiae, satire, etc.
I. Title.
PN6231.A5S713   1981   838'.91407   81-10429
ISBN 0-226-77895-9 (pbk.)   AACR2

56,968

CONTENTS

INTRODUCTION

Among mammals the order SNOUTERS holds an
unique position, to be explained first of all by the fact
that these most oddly constructed animals have been discovered only very recently. That hitherto they have remained unknown to science is because their native land,
the South Sea Archipelago Hy-yi-yi (written Heieiei in
German), was not discovered until the year 1941 and
even then was visited for the first time by civilized Euro-
peans through a rare chance connected with the Pacific
war. But in addition this group of animals has particular
significance because among them are found principles of
structure, modes of behavior, and ecological types that
are unknown elsewhere, not just among mammals but
among vertebrates in general.

Discovery of the archipelago is to be credited to the
Swede Einar Pettersson-Skämtkvist who—escaping from
Japanese imprisonment—was wrecked on the island Hy-
dud-dye-fee (Heidadaifi). This island, which in contrast
to many islands of the South Seas is not of volcanic
origin even though it does not lack an active volcano
(Kotsobousi-Kozobausi) of respectable height (5740
feet), extends some twenty miles from north to south
and about ten miles east to west, consists predominantly
of limestone and metamorphic shales, and has as its

highest elevation Shou-wunoonda (Schauanunda), a twin-peaked mountain 7316 feet high. The climate of the island is extremely equable, as is customary of islands of the central and eastern Pacific. The tropical vegetation, the botanical evaluation of which has scarcely begun, displays alongside genera of worldwide distribution many endemic forms of archaic character (thus the Maierales, closely related to the Psilotales; and the genus *Neolepidodendron,* to be classed among the Lepidodendrales; and likewise the Schultzeales, that form a series of magnificent virgin forest trees and that are to be ranked near the Ranunculaceae; and many more). The Hy-yi-yi Archipelago, to which Hy-dud-dye-fee belongs, must hence be of ancient origin, as is true also in respect to the geological-palaeontological findings (almost exclusively palaeozoic deposits; cf. *Classification of the Miliolid Sands from the Upper Horizon D16 of Mairúvili* by Ezio Sputalave. At the very latest, the island group must have become completely isolated from other continents in the Upper Cretaceous; likewise it is to be assumed that the archipelago, for its part, is the remnant of a fair-sized continent, since—in contrast to New Zealand—it contains an incomparably greater variety and peculiarity of native groups of organisms on a total island area of only slightly more than 650 square miles.

The natives found by Skämtkvist on his arrival in 1941 called themselves Hooakha-Hutchi (Huacha-Hatschi). They have since become extinct, but according to Skämtkvist seem to have been polynesian-europaeoid. It was impossible to investigate their language because a headcold introduced by the discoverer destroyed these children of nature inside of a few months. Of their cultural artifacts only a few wooden objects could be saved

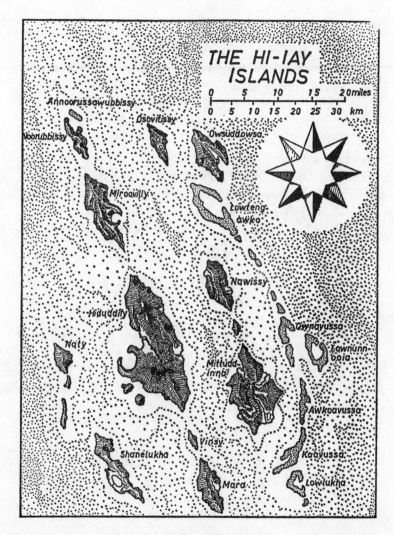

PLATE I

(cf. also Deuterich 1944 and Combinatore 1943). Weapons were unknown to the Hooakha-Hutchi. The peaceful tribe was supported by the natural bounty of the surroundings. There was no excess of births; rather, "from time immemorial" twenty-two chiefs had held sway over approximately seven hundred souls. This much Skämtkvist was able to ascertain. These astute arrangements had the fortunate scientific byproduct that despite the presence of humankind the extraordinary archipelagic world of organisms was preserved, as is the more astounding because almost all the terrestrial animals would have been destroyed if they had been hunted more intensively.

Despite the fact that their native home was unknown, Snouters had been mentioned on one previous occasion. No lesser personage than the poet Christian Morgenstern some sixty years ago announced the existence of the Snouters in his well-known poem:

> "Along on its probosces
> there goes the nasobame[1]
> accompanied by its young one.
> It is not found in Brehm,[*]
> It is not found in Meyer,[**]
> Nor in the Brockhaus[**] anywhere.
> 'Twas only through my lyre
> we knew it had been there.
> Thenceforth on its probosces
> (above I've said the same)
> accompanied by its offspring
> there goes the nasobame."

[1] *nasus* Lat.=nose; *Bēma* Grk.=to walk.

[*] classical German treatise on zoology, first edition 1863, fourth (last) edition 1918.

[**] names of well-known German encyclopedias.

This concise and yet clear description, that expresses the peculiar gait of this Snouter even in the rhythm of the verse, answers to a hair that of *Nasobema lyricum*.[2] Hence one cannot think other than that Morgenstern must have had a specimen of this Snouter before him or have had detailed information about it. Bleedkoop 1945 in *Das Nasobemproblem* (*The Nasobame Problem*) considers that there are two possibilities. Either Morgenstern was briefly in Hy-yi-yi during the years 1893 to 1897, or through some chance or other he received a hide of *Nasobema lyricum* (the *hónatata* of the natives). Yet no tropical expedition of Morgenstern's is known, and how might he have obtained a hide? According to a verbal communication from Mrs. Käthe Züller, with whom Morgenstern was well acquainted, he is said to have come home one evening in 1894 in the greatest excitement, muttering over and over "Hy-yi-yi, Hy-yi-yi!" Soon thereafter, it is said, he composed the poem in question, which he also showed her brother. Bleedkoop concludes from this that Morgenstern had learned of Hy-yi-yi from an acquaintance. But whether he actually had the *hónatata* before him, or with a poet's intuition simply sketched a picture of the animal, must remain enigmatic. The lines: "'Twas only through my lyre we knew it had been there" would permit the deduction that he didn't actually see it, but knew of it only by description. Perhaps too he wished to veil the islands with their ancient organisms from European greed and hence—to an extent as camouflage—wove these lines into his poem? We do not know, just as we do not know from whom Morgenstern got his information about Hy-yi-yi and its fauna. Actually the only possibility in this direction is a merchant sailor, Captain Albrecht Jens Miespott, who

---

[2] *lyricus* Grk.=pertaining to the lyre.

died at an early age; Morgenstern maintained a considerable correspondence with him. In 1894, after returning from a long and extraordinary journey, Miespott died in a state of mental derangement in Hamburg. Perhaps it was he who knew the secret of Hy-yi-yi and carried it with him to the grave. So much for Bleedkoop's investigations.

In a meritorious study I. I. Schutliwitzkij occupied himself with the same problem. He comes to about the same conclusion as Bleedkoop, but with the difference that he considers it possible that between the years 1894 and 1896 Morgenstern received from Miespott's estate a living *hónatata*, that he kept in a cigar box for some weeks. Yet here too the data are contradictory. Moreover, it could have been no more than a "pouch-baby," since *hónatatas* grow to a respectable size (cf. p. 55). All that is certain is that the cigar box was quite a deep one, labeled *"Los selectos hediondos de desecho."*

GENERAL

The Snouters, which are regarded as a special order of
the mammals, and which have found a monographer in
the well-known specialist Bromeante de Burlas, are—
as the name indicates—all distinguished by the fact that
the snout is extraordinarily developed. It may be present
singly, or in a greater number. The latter condition is
unique among the vertebrates. Now, anatomical investigations (here we follow Bromeante de Burlas' discus-
sions) have shown that in the polyrrhine species the nasal
rudiment is cleft at an early embryonic stage, so that the
rudimentary individual nostrils that develop from it have
a holorrhinous differentiation, i.e. each forms a complete
snout (cf. Fig. 1). Together with the early polyrrhinali-
zation there occur numerous extensive alterations of the
entire structural plan of the head. Special muscles, derived from the facial musculature (innervated by the
N. facialis or by a branch, the *N. nasuloambulacralis*,[3]
that is unusually well-developed here) take part in the
musculation of the snout. Beyond this, in one group (the
hopsorrhines[4] or Snout Leapers) the capacity of the

[3] *nasulus* Lat.=a little nose; *ambulare* Lat.=to walk.
[4] *hopsos* Grk.=a jump or leap (a word, found only in Chrysostomos
of Massilia, that apparently is to be traced back to a West Germanic
root) ; *rhis, rhinós* Grk.=a nose.

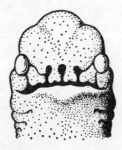

[Fig. 1] *Nasobema lyricum.* Head of a young embryo, to show the polyrrhine condition (after Stultén 1949).

snout to develop energy is increased further by *M. longissimus dorsi,* which is drawn out forwards over the skull. The nasal sinuses and the *corpora spongiosa* undergo far-reaching alteration and an increase in size, which are accompanied by a shift in function. Thus for instance in almost all of the more advanced forms the tear duct takes on the functions of an outer respiratory passage. Such special details will be considered further in discussing the individual species.

Inasmuch as in these rhinograde animals—with exception of the genus *Archirrhinus* (a Primitive Snouter) —the *nasarium*[5] serves as a means of progression, the other appendages have lost their locomotory functions. Correspondingly, the posterior appendages are mostly more or less reduced, while the anterior appendages have been modified as grasping organs for holding the food or as little hands for grooming. In the genus

[5] Bromeante de Burlas designates as *nasarium* the entirety of the rhinal *ambulacrum,* irrespective of the origin of its components. Hence *"nasarium"* is a functional rather than a morphological concept. Since this term has become entrenched in the literature and its use avoids the necessity of lengthy descriptions, it will be employed throughout the passages that follow.

Rhinostentor (Trumpet Snouters) they participate in the formation of a water-filtering apparatus.

Whereas, then, the paired appendages are less impressive features of the general organization of the Snouters, with these animals the tail occupies an outstanding place and in its construction has developed manifold and altogether aberrant types. Thus one finds not only coiling tails and lasso-like tails, but also in the sclerorrhines[6] (the Proboscipedes) the tail serves the more primitive forms for jumping and the more advanced ones as a grasping organ (cf. pp. 35, 36, and 48).

In most Snouters the body is covered with a fairly uniform coat, in which no distinction can be made between underfur and guard hairs; this is to be attributed not only to the climatic conditions of the archipelago, but according to Bromeante de Burlas is to be regarded as a primitive character. This view is favored also by the regular way in which the hairs are grouped. In one genus there are in addition strong horny scales (similar to those of scaly anteaters), that are altogether of the nature of reptilian scales. At times the coloration of the coat is magnificent. Famous above all is the extraordinary luster of the pelt, caused by the special structure of the hair cortex. The bare spots too—head, feet, tail, ears, combs of skin on the head and especially on the snout—are brilliantly colored at times. A few aquatic species, and the very small burrowing species that are found on the sandy shore, are completely bare; likewise a single parasitic species (cf. p. 19).

The manner of feeding varies greatly among the different families, and even within the same family or genus. Yet this is hardly surprising when one recalls that besides

---

[6] *sklerós* Grk.=hard.

a single aquatic shrew[7] the Snouters are the only mammals of the archipelago and have thus been able to take possession of all ecological niches. Most of the rhinograde animals, the average size of which is indeed small, eat insects. But in addition there are also herbivores—especially fructivorous species—and one predacious genus. To be mentioned finally as particularly specialized forms are the plankton feeders that live in fresh water, and the burrowing forms, among which are the tiniest vertebrates known. The crab-eaters among the hopsorrhines can be derived readily from the insectivorous forms. A strange case of symbiosis will be discussed in the systematic section (pp. 15, 37).

It is particularly remarkable that among the Snouters there is one flying genus (with a single species), and that there are also sessile and parasitic forms. Considering the habits and the structural organization of the animals, however, one is not astonished that the number of species is rather large. In this connection geological interest is attached to the excellent study by M. O. Jester and S. P. Assfugl of the genus *Dulcicauda*[8] (the Honeytails). These authors were able to show that land bridges must have persisted for various lengths of time between the different islands of the archipelago, and were able to estimate the dates of their interruption (cf. also Ludwig 1954). All in all, the study with this material of *Rassenkreise* and their evolution (Rensch 1947) is especially

---

[7] *Limnogaloides mairuviliensis* B. d. B. (the Mairúvilian swamp shrew) is a primitive insectivore. That it belongs to the true shrews has recently been contested. On this account too the earlier name *Limnosorex mairuviliensis* has come into disuse. The dental formula, the well-developed zygomatic arch, the unusually small forebrain, and the presence of intervertebral muscles along the entire length of the tail are regarded as especially primitive characters.

[8] *dulcis* Lat.=sweet; *cauda* Lat.=tail.

promising, even though in many areas there are great gaps that are hardly to be closed even by the palaeontological approach, since the pertinent fossils lie in deposits that have sunk beneath the surface of the sea.

In general the reproductivity of the Snouters is not high, which permits the conclusion that the death rate also is low. So far as now is known there is invariably a single young at a birth (the Snout Leapers with physiological polyembryony are an exception). However, pregnant females occur all year long. The period of gestation —again with exception of the Snout Leapers—is long and lasts seven months on the average. Among the monorrhine forms the young are so advanced in development at birth that they do not have to be suckled. Correlatively, the mammary glands of these Snouters are vestigial or display, in the genus *Columnifax*[9] (Pillar Snouters), lactation independent of a lactation hormone (cf. p. 15). In the polyrrhine genera, in which the newborn are in quite a dependent condition, there is a single pair of (mostly axillary) teats. As a rule these species also possess a brood pouch, that is formed of skin folds on the throat and is supported by cartilaginous bars descending from the Adam's apple.

The rhinogrades have scarcely any enemies. In the interior of the islands the only warm-blooded creatures besides the already mentioned swamp shrew (*Limnogaloides*) are birds of the genus *Hypsiboas*[10] (Megaphone Birds). All these are of the size of songbirds and have occupied biotopes quite distinct from those of the Rhinogradentia. According to Bouffon and Schprimarsch they are descended from petrels, and in fact from forms

---

[9] *columna* Lat.=pillar; *fax* Lat.=-making.
[10] *hypsibóas* Grk.=loud crier (Doric form of Attic *hypsiboes*).

close to *Hydrobates*. Reptiles are lacking. There occurs only a single primitive amphibian species (*Urobombinator submersus*[11]), whose gigantic larvae are devoured by the Hooakha-Hutchi at ceremonial feasts. The slow-moving *Nasobema* species have enemies from their own ranks in the predacious rhinogrades of the genus Tyrannonasus.[12] However, this genus is confined to a few islands. For the most part, only the oceanic birds that at certain seasons breed on some of the smaller islands occasionally take a rhinograde. However, those very species (for instance the Honeytails and the Pillar Snouters) that live on the shore are protected from the birds' attacks, in part by poison devices and in part by being inedible; and the Snout Leapers are in general so agile that they are not to be caught by these birds.

Here attention may be called to yet another peculiarity of the Hy-yi-yi-an fauna: the insects display a great number of very primitive forms. Thus the cockroach-like kinds are represented by numerous structurally distinct types, most of which can be placed among the Blattariae. Besides these there are also a few more advanced insects, above all Hymenoptera, whereas Lepidoptera are absent altogether. Hence, pollination is accomplished partly by Hymenoptera (above all by the *Pseudobombus* species, that outwardly resemble bumblebees but that actually are related to the xylocopids), and partly by caddisflies and cockroaches. There are no ants. As a marked peculiarity the six-winged insects (Hexaptera of the superorder Hexapteroidea[13]) should be mentioned; they are descendants of the Palaeodictyoptera and have terrestrial larvae. These insects are mostly

---

[11] *ura* Grk.=tail; *bombina* Lat.=toad; *submersus* Lat.=submerged.
[12] tyrant-nose.
[13] six-winged insects.

animals of the open country; i.e. except for a few species they avoid the thick virgin forests that clothe the mountain slopes of the larger islands. Here too we may record the peculiarity that the larger islands have some endemic species. These primitive forms are wholly lacking in the smaller islands. Probably this is to be attributed to the fact that the smaller islands (for instance Ownavussa or Sawabisi) are coral islands and hence of recent formation, or because they do not afford sufficient protection against the wind for inept fliers, so that any endemic species there died out as the islands sank and grew smaller.

With respect to the systematic arrangement of the Snouters, the following considerations apply:

As shown by the single species that still walks on all four legs (genus: *Archirrhinos*=Primitive Snouters), they must have been derived from primitive insectivores. In this connection the presence on Mairúvili of *Limnogaloides* is significant; for this animal, that unquestionably is to be reckoned among the Insectivora, has many features in common with *Archirrhinos,* so that it is not impossible that both species may be traced back to a common ancestry.

For the rest, the systematic classification of the Snouters follows predominantly the degree of development of the snout. The "family tree" in Fig. 2, showing the systematic subdivisions of the order, was proposed by Bromeante de Burlas (1950). According to it he distinguishes as principal groups Uni-Snouters that walk on legs=*Monorrhina pedestria* (with *Archirrhinus haeckelii* as the sole species), Uni-Snouters that walk on the snout=*Monorrhina nasestria* (with Soft-nosed Snouters =*Asclerorrhina* and Proboscipedes=*Sclerorrhina*), and Multi-Snouters=*Polyrrhina* (with Short-nosed Snouters

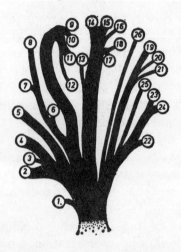

[Fig. 2] Proposed family tree of the individual genera of the
Rhinogradentia (modified from Bromeante de Burlas, with the
help of Stultén's data).
1. *Archirrhinos;* 2. *Nasolimaceus;* 3. *Emunctator;*
4. *Dulcicauda;* 5. *Columnifax;* 6. *Rhinotaenia;*
7. *Rhinosiphonia;* 8. *Rhinostentor;* 9. *Rhinotalpa;*
10. *Enterorrhinus;* 11. *Holorrhinus;* 12. *Remanonasus;*
13. *Phyllohoppla;* 14. *Hopsorrhinus;* 15. *Mercatorrhinus;*
16. *Otopteryx;* 17. *Orchidiopsis;* 18. *Liliopsis;* 19. *Nasobema;*
20. *Stella;* 21. *Tyrannonasus;* 22. *Eledonopsis;* 23. *Hexanthus;*
24. *Cephalantus;* 25. *Mammontops;* 26. *Rhinochilopus.* The
thickness of the branches indicates the relative numbers of
species of the several genera. Here *Dulcicauda* and *Dulcidauca*
that elsewhere are regarded as separate genera are placed
together under *Dulcicauda.*

=*Brachyproata* and Long-nosed Snouters=*Dolichoproata*). Whereas most genera can be accommodated without difficulty in this scheme, it is still uncertain with regard to the Mole Snouters=*Rhinotalpiformes* whether
they can be united in a single group with the Burrowing

Snouters=*Hypogeonasida*,[14] or whether they have been derived from the *Sclerorrhina* (Proboscipedes) and possess a secondarily expanded *nasarium*.

The 14 families contain altogether 189 species; there is still a possibility that one or another unknown species inhabits some isolated region of the archipelago. This may be anticipated the more because the just-mentioned group of the Rhinotalpiformes has yielded surprising discoveries of new types in recent years. Some systematic difficulties are to be expected also when the question is clarified for broadly distributed species as to when we are dealing with true races, i.e. genetically distinct populations, and when merely with local modifications. The example of *Mammontops*[15] (Shaggy-faced Snouters), that originally was native to Shou-wunoonda and later was kept by the Naval Administration in the zoo at the experimental station on Shay-nay-lukha (Schenelacha), demonstrated the extraordinary degree to which the phenotype could be modified. Genetic experiments have failed hitherto because of the difficulty of rearing the animals (cf. p. xix). Only *Hopsorrhinus* once again affords an exception. However, here experiment has shown that the different island forms are true—though closely related—species. Only when *Hopsorrhinus aureus* (the Golden Snout Leaper) from Mitadina was crossed with *Hopsorrhinus macrohopsus*[16] (Pike's Snout Leaper) from Hy-dud-dye-fee were there a few of the offspring with a limited capacity for reproduction. *Hopsorrhinus*

[14] *hypo* Grk.=under; *gea* Grk.=earth.

[15] *mamont*, Russ., borrowed from Palaeosiberian languages=mammoth. The spelling *mammonta* is intrinsically erroneous, but correct according to the rules of nomenclature. *-ops* Grk.=face. In the figure (Fig. 2) the spelling accepted in the years 1952–56 has been used.

[16] *makrós* Grk.=big; *hopsos* cf. Footnote 4.

mercator[17] (=*Mercatorrhinus galactophilus*,[18] Healey's Snout Leaper) too has proved favorable for genetic experimentation; with a gestation period of only eighteen days it usually bears eight young of a single sex and is very readily maintained on commercially obtainable condensed milk for babies (cf. p. 37).

[17] *mercator* Lat.=a merchant.
[18] *galacto-philus* Grk.=fond of milk.

THE SNOUTERS

DESCRIPTION OF THE SEVERAL
GROUPS

SUBORDER: Monorrhina (Uni-Snouters),
SECTION: Pedestria (Foot-Walkers),
TRIBE: Archirrhiniformes (Primitive Snouter Types),
FAMILY: Archirrhinidae (Primitive Snouters *sens. lat.*),
1 GENUS: *Archirrhinos* (Primitive Snouters proper),
1 Species.

Archirrhinos haeckelii (Haeckel's Primitive Snouter) is
the only living representative of the Primitive Snouters.*
It still walks on four legs like other mammals, and still
lacks a highly differentiated *nasarium*. Thus the snout is
altogether unadapted to function as a locomotory organ
and merely serves the animal as a support when it is

* In contrast with all other Snouters, fossils are known of *Archirrhinos* or of closely related forms. On the island Owsa-dowsa (Ausa-
dausa), that is tectonically exceptional in the archipelago, there are
Early Tertiary deposits that might perhaps be assigned in part to the
Upper Cretaceous also. In excavations of these there have been found
teeth of an archirrhine that must have been the size of a house cat.

1

Archirrhinos haeckelii

PLATE II

devouring captured prey (cf. Plate II, animal in background). The habits of the Primitive Snouter resemble in many respects those of a shrew: whereas in the daytime it sleeps in a simple nest under roots, at twilight it emerges in search of food. Then the mouse-sized creature with its thick head and enormous snout may be seen running about and chasing the huge cockroaches, large numbers of which often are gathered around the banana-shaped berries that have fallen at the foot of the *Wisoleka* trunks. When a Snouter has caught an insect, it dives swiftly onto the snout, the margins of which spread quickly apart to form a broad supporting surface. Viscous nasal mucus provides firm hold of the ground. And now the greedy beast brings the food very rapidly to its mouth with all four feet. From afar the feasting creatures betray their presence with loud chattering squeaks. Once the meal is done they reverse from their headstand just as quickly, the margins of the snout are rolled inward again, and the chase is resumed. Little is known as yet about the reproduction of these animals, since they occur only in the inaccessible mountain forests of Hy-dud-dye-fee.

SUBORDER: Monorrhina (Uni-Snouters),
SECTION: Nasestria (Snout-Walkers),
TRIBE: Asclerorrhina (Soft-nosed Snouters),
SUBTRIBE: Epigeonasida[19] (Surface Snouters),
FAMILY: Nasolimacidae[20] (Snail-like Snouters),
GENUS: *Nasolimaceus* (Slime Snouters),
4 Species,*

GENUS: *Rhinolimaceus* (Sugarmice),
14 Species.

The monorrhine Nasestria, with the tribe Asclerorrhina, are closely related to the archirrhines. Without exception they are animals in which the modifications of the nasal region made in connection with an altered mode of locomotion have remained within narrow limits. The significant features comprise enlargement of the snout and of those parts of the skull that serve to support it. However, the following structural peculiarities are to be regarded as new developments: multiple subdivision of the muscles of the snout, and of the nasal sinuses,

[19] *Epi* Grk.=upon; *gea* cf. Footnote 14.
[20] *limax* Lat.=a snail.
* Here, as in subsequent sections, only a single especially typical representative is named and described. For detailed data reference is made to the work by Bromeante de Burlas (1951) and to the somewhat shorter monograph by J. D. Bitbrain (1950).

whereby is formed a system of air chambers that intercommunicate but that can be closed off from one another by special muscles; further the marked development of the *corpora spongiosa,* that provide the snout with the turgor essential for its functions. In most species this can be varied at will. Besides, the muscles of those portions of the face adjacent to the snout are in part extended over the snout itself and differentiated extensively so that the snout (which according to Bitbrain is already a true *nasarium*) has gained considerable flexibility. A further characteristic is the great expansion of the secretory epithelium, the voluntarily regulated mucus production of which is important for the locomotion of the animals and for their fastening themselves securely in place.

As already mentioned in the General Section, the appendages are reduced or modified. The hindlegs are vestigial (but are never lacking entirely) and are practically without function. The anterior appendages serve both for seizing the food and for grooming.

Nasolimaceus palustris[21] (the Fadelacha Slime Snouter) will be described as a typical representative of the nasolimacids. It is also most closely related to *Archirrhinos.* This approximately mouse-sized creature, with a vivid golden-brown pelt, occurs on Mairúvili and there inhabits the muddy banks of the Fadelacha. It has a short but broad snout, the anteriorly directed ventral surface of which is modified as a creeping foot and functions much like the foot of *Helix,* with the difference however that the locomotory waves of contraction succeed one another more rapidly and are reversible. The speed of translation is greater than would be expected from the mechanism of movement. When the animal is

[21] *palustris* Lat.=marsh-inhabiting.

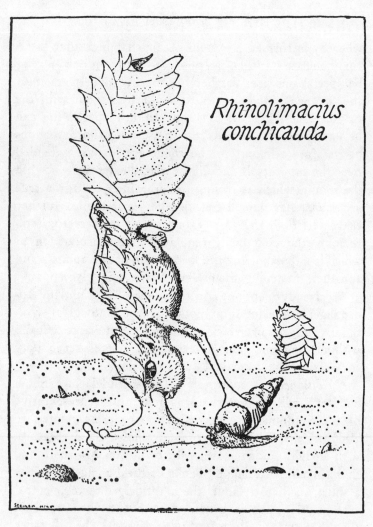

Rhinolimacius conchicauda

PLATE III

in flight or is chasing something it will cover some 35–40 ft/min. Under such circumstances it seems to glide with almost ghostly speed over the smooth damp mud; and the precise mode of progression is no longer to be followed by eye but can be recorded only by high-speed photography. An impressive motion picture of this has been made recently by F. Hyderitsch of the Scientific and Medical Cinematographic Company, Black Goats. Snails of an endemic genus (*Ankelella*) furnish the sole food of the *Nasolimaceus* species; only *Rhinolimaceus fodiens*,[22] known to the sailors of the marine base as "Lucky Pierre," digs out earthworms (that in part belong to the same genera as the endemic earthworms of New Zealand!). Before they lose their "baby teeth," the young feed mostly on larval insects (chironomids), inasmuch as they are not yet able to cope with the hard snail shells.

Mating, during which the male occasionally utters sounds as though he were blowing his nose, takes place mostly at night. Then the male dashes in tight curves around the female, who also is rotating. From time to time she too emits a gentle "Hm-hm." The stage for these games of love is usually a large flat stone that is coated with a thin, slimy layer of diatoms and over which the water occasionally purls besides. The affair as a whole has a grotesque resemblance to the dancing of a human couple on ice skates. The act of mating lasts but a few seconds, and then the partners forsake one another, going very rapidly in opposite directions with a sound as of gentle nose-blowing. After gestation of twenty-six (?) months the female bears a single offspring that already resembles the parents in all details and that,

[22] *fodiens* Lat.=burrowing.

without further dependence on them, undertakes a life of its own.

The animals do not patrol a constant range; they lead strictly solitary lives and are tolerant of one another. In general, as Snail-like Snouters that are adapted to muddy fresh-water beaches, they are confined to the bodies of water where they were born, since they can neither swim nor will willingly cross extended stretches of other than muddy or sandy substrates. Despite this, from time to time one comes upon immature specimens—whose appendages at this stage still are relatively more strongly developed—wandering slowly overland in a search for other bodies of water. The animals cannot withstand sea water—like many other Snouters—and on this account it is understandable that there are numerous specific variations on different islands.

Closely related to *Nasolimaceus palustris* is *Nasolimaceus conchicauda*[23] (the Armor-tailed slime Snouter). This animal that as its name implies has an armored tail, lives on the little volcanic islet Eeza-zofa (Isasofa), on the marsh of the same name. By bending its tail ventrad beneath it the animal can conceal itself in it as though in a beach chair. It is significant that Eeza-zofa is inhabited by a hypsiboant that poses a threat to the Snouter. This is the flightless *Hypsiboas fritschii* (Fritsch's Megaphone Bird), an adept runner and swimmer the size of a thrush, that feeds upon practically all animals it can catch and overcome.

The remaining nasolimacids are well protected against enemies by the fact that at the base of the tail they have a gland that gives off a sweet secretion (whence the name

[23] *conche* Grk.=a shell or shield; *cauda* Lat. cf. Footnote 8.

"Sugarmouse"). The fluid attracts a very small *Pseudobombus* species, that is extremely ready to sting; for the most part the Sugarmice are attended by swarms of these insects and hence are protected.*

* According to studies by Shirin Tafarruj the glandular secretion contains only small amounts of glucose but in addition to them a sweet substance the constitution of which has still not been fully determined; structurally this is close neither to dulcin nor to saccharin and in pure form is some 200-times more stimulating than saccharin. It is noteworthy that this material has approximately equal sweetness for people and for the insect.

FAMILY: Rhinocolumnidae (Pillar-nosed Snouters
sens. lat.),
GENUS: *Emunctator* (Snifflers),
1 Species,

GENUS: *Dulcicauda* (Honeytails),
19 Species,

GENUS: Dulcidauca[24] (Sugartails),
1 Species,

GENUS: *Columnifax* (Pillar-nosed Snouters proper)
11 Species.

The position of the rhinolimacids in classification is still disputed: whereas Spasman and Stultén as late as 1947 still maintained that they were to be placed in a special Section (Sedentaria) opposite the Peripatetica, today people mostly follow Bromeante de Burlas and include them in the subtribe Epigeonasida. The principal reason for this is the discovery of *Emunctator sorbens* (the Snuffling Sniffler), that occupies a place intermediate between the errant rhinolimacids and the sedentary rhinocolumnids.

On the other hand it is not impossible that the rhinocolumnids are a polyphyletic group. Bouffon (1954) only recently has once again pointed out that there are radical

[24] *Dulcidauca:* an anagram of *Dulcicauda,* cf. Footnote 8.

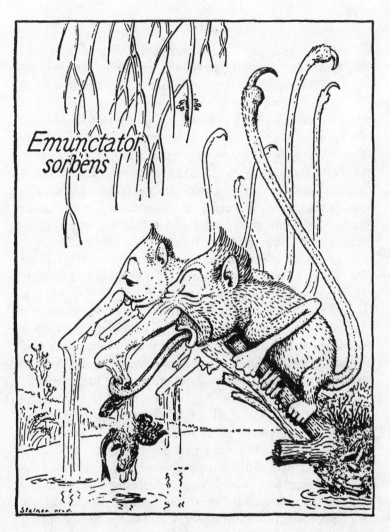

Emunctator sorbens

PLATE IV

differences between *Emunctator* and *Dulcicauda* on the one hand and *Columnifax* on the other: 1. the innervation of the hyporrhinal musculature is fundamentally different in the two groups; and 2. the substances found in the column base (the pedestal on which *Dulcicauda* and *Columnifax* stand) are in part very distinct. The prehensile threads of *Emunctator* and the supporting base of *Dulcicauda* both contain the so-called "*Emunctator*-mucin," that has in it a pentose-containing mucoid sulphuric acid which is lacking in *Columnifax*. On the other hand, the *Columnifax* pedestal contains a pseudorhinokeratin that does not occur in the other genera.

The Snuffling Sniffler, *Emunctator sorbens* (cf. Plate IV), is an animal about the size of a small rat. It lives on Hy-dud-dye-fee along the banks of slowly flowing brooks. There it clings to the stalks of plants that rise above the surface. Its manner of obtaining nourishment is most peculiar: from the elongate snout it blows long, fine prehensile threads that hang down into the water and to which little aquatic animals get stuck. The prey (mainly copepods and larval insects, but also isopods and amphipods, and less often small fish) is in part ingested choanally by pulling up the slimy threads, and is in part licked off the snout by the extremely long tongue.

The sluggish, dull animals possess, as a means of defense, a long, very mobile tail with a poison gland at the tip; the toxin is secreted into a hollow claw (derived from modified hairs). Since *Emunctator* lives for the most part in small groups, the little creatures can protect one another by mutual tail-wagging.

As a typical representative of the genus *Dalcicauda*, *D. griseaurella* (the Greyish-Golden Honeytail) will be described (here as in what follows the names assigned by Bromeante de Burlas will be used, and hence the name of

Dulcicauda griseaurella

Steiner pinx.

PLATE V

the original author usually is not given). This species, together with *D. aromaturus* (the Perfumed Honeytail) is found on Mitadina, *D. griseaurella* in the eastern and *D. aromaturus* in the western half of the island.

The odd thing about these animals is that they are true sedentary forms that stand fast on their snouts and normally never forsake the place of attachment that they have chosen when young. Thus they remain supported on the snout, that gives off a reddish-yellow secretion which in time elevates the creatures (head+torso ca. 3 in. long, tail about 4 in.) on a conspicuous, pillar-shaped pedestal, known as the base or *sella* (cf. Plate V). Especially toward the tip, that bears a poison-claw, the tail has a wealth of dermal glands, that secrete a fruity, sticky product. Insects attracted to settle on the tail by the fragrance thus given out, stick to it and are picked off by the forepaws and brought to the mouth. At times, when the insects landing mostly are small they are not collected individually from the tail, but from time to time the animal pulls the tail through the mouth and licks them off.

Dulcicauda lives in colonies on rubbly slopes near the shore. These colonies regularly are associated with a small land crab (*Chestochele*[25] *marmorata*), that feeds on scraps from the Snouters' meals and carries away their droppings.

At mating time the males descend from their pedestals and approach the females, slipping and sliding along with their forelegs in advance; once copulation has been accomplished they return to their pedestals. They are enabled to free themselves from the base of their column

---

[25] *chestón* Grk.=dung (in Euphémios Thereutes of Alexandria); *chele* Grk.=a cleft claw, crab's pincers.

through a partial dissolution of its uppermost layers by means of enzymes given out by Pusdiva's glands of the *discus nasalis* (the same is true in regard to the dissolution of the fastening mucus in *Archirrhinos*).

The genus *Columnifax* is distinguished in general by a reduction in length of the prehensile tail. On this account the animals are unable to catch their own prey. Only young specimens, not yet three months old, still have a relatively long, secretory tail and still nourish themselves in the same way as *Dulcicauda* or *Dulcidauca* (*Dulcidauca* is characterized by loss of the posterior appendages). With older individuals there is established a most noteworthy symbiosis with a hopsorrhinid: each of the eleven *Columnifax* species is associated with one of the eleven subspecies of *Hopsorrhinos mercator* (Healey's Snout Leaper). The two partners are rigidly dependent on one another, and see to each others' nourishment: in the littoral zone where the two live the predominant booty of *Hopsorrhinus mercator* is small hermit crabs which, however, it is unable to ingest because of its oral modifications (cf. p. 37). Hence it turns them over to the Pillar Snouter after it has suppressed the latter's defense reactions by means of definite sounds and gestures. (*Columnifax* defends itself by squirting out a secretion from anal stink glands, and with its very mobile snout is able to twist some 180° about the long axis). Thereupon *Columnifax* permits the hopsorrhinid to suckle; in connection with the described symbiosis, milk is produced by individuals of both sexes, when over three months old, without reference to any sexual function (cf. Plate VII).

SUBTRIBE: Hypogeonasida (Mud Snouters),
FAMILY: Rhinosiphonidae (Siphon Snouters
sens. lat.),
GENUS: *Rhinotaenia* (Ribbon Snouters),
2 Species,

GENUS: *Rhinosiphonia* (Siphon Snouters proper),
3 Species,

FAMILY: Rhinostentoridae (Trumpet Snouters
sens. lat.),
GENUS: *Rhinostentor* (Trumpet Snouters proper),
3 Species

The Hypogeonasida too are in themselves a relatively isolated group. They are all small unimpressive animals with originally a subterranean way of life that is most typically developed in the genus *Rhinotaenia*. As a characteristic representative *Rhinotaenia asymmetrica* (the Snorkeling Ribbon Snouter) will next be described.

[Fig. 3] Rhinotaenia asymmetrica. (Orig.)

This animal lives in the mud of a few small lakes as in the supralittoral regions of a few gently flowing streams. There it feeds principally upon oligochaetes and larval insects, that it digs out and gulps down with its long, proboscis-like mouth. In doing this, *Rhinotaenia* daily digs itself forward one or two yards at a depth of about a foot. Respiration is made possible by the long nose, that is extended siphon-like as much as 16 in.— i.e. up to some four times the length of the animal's head and body (cf. Fig. 3). The asymmetry of the snout —the left nostril with its terminal rosette serves for inhalation and the right for exhaling—affords a perfect supply of air, despite the length of the air tubes.

Nothing is known regarding mating and reproduction. Pregnant females and very small young are to be found all year long.

Beilig was able to extract from isolated *Rhinotaenia* snouts a mucin that is identical with that of *Emunctator*. Morphologically too much can be advanced in favor of the view that the hypogeonasids derive from *Emunctator*-like ancestors (cf. Bromeante de Burlas 1952 as well as Jerker and Celiazzini 1953).

The genus *Rhinosiphonia* differs from *Rhinotaenia* primarily in the finer construction of the snout, but does not offer any further distinctions from *Rhinotaenia* that require comment here. Instead we may discuss here one *Rhinotaenia* species that is unique in its peculiar parasitic habits.

Rhinotaenia tridacnae (the Shell-inhabiting Ribbon Snouter; cf. Fig. 4) is found in the tidal zone throughout the archipelago. The young animals and the males live in mud that is deposited in still portions of the lagoons or that collects in little clefts between the blocks of coral. Even more than with the rest of the Rhinogradentia

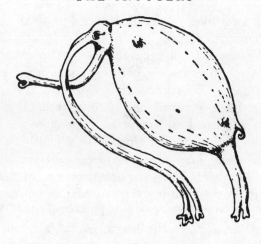

[Fig. 4] Rhinotaenia tridacnae, shown at the age of sexual maturity.

Note the reduction of the paired extremities as well as the anal and urogenital orifices. The head is remarkable for its small size, for the nasal orifice and oral proboscus, and for the importance of the tear ducts situated in front of the regressive eyes. (Orig.)

and especially with the hypogeonasids, homoiothermy is only very incompletely developed with *Rhinotaenia tridacnae*. Connected with this is the fact that *R. tridacnae* will for a considerable time withstand a more or less complete interruption of oxidative metabolism. Of course the creatures live in the upper tidal zone, the mud of which is inundated for only from a quarter- to half-an-hour at a time. Yet these animals can withstand being cut off from atmospheric air for as much as three hours. They then fall into a kind of fit and—bareskinned as they are—turn blue over the whole body, to regain a yellowish flesh color as soon as they inhale air once more.

Now at high tide the mature *R. tridacnae* females enter the open shells of the genus *Tridacna* (Giant Mussels) and burrow very swiftly down between the shell and the mantle. There they soon cause a swelling of the mantle about as large as a fist or a child's head, only a part of which, however, delaminates mother-of-pearl; at low tide this growth is filled with air by the mussel and projects like a hernia into the gill space. With its suctorial proboscis the parasite takes in from the host both hemolymph and a part of the sexual products. Mating with the *Rhinotaenia* males takes place at flood tide at night. Apparently the young also are born at flood tide at night.

The rhinostentorids are closely related to *Rhinotaenia*, but have become adapted to a submerged life and hence have undergone some modifications* that are expressed most typically in *Rhinostentor submersus*[26] (the Cladoceran-like Trumpet Snouter).

Rhinostentor submersus lives in various crater lakes and brackish lagoons in the archipelago, and feeds there on plankton, to wit principally on the leaf-footed crab, *Branchipusiops lacustris*, that for the most part occurs here in numbers that only occasionally are reduced by the ubiquitous Cladocera or Rotatoria. Here *Rhinostentor* hangs, at a depth of 8–20 in., from a nasal siphon that is constructed in general like that of *Rhinotaenia* but that, in correlation with an aquatic habit, exhibits an expansion of the nasal rosette. The rosette grows funnel-like around the outgoing nasal passage, while the afferent nasal passage is raised above it to form a small secondary rosette. The funnel-shaped or trumpet-shaped

* Here there is no attempt at an explanation in the sense of Böker, but merely a record of the observations.
[26] cf. Footnote 7.

[Fig. 5] Rhinostentor submersus. (Orig.)

nasal rosette (cf. Fig. 5) is fringed with water-repellent
hairs and at the margins (modified wax glands) gives off
a water-repellent, wax-like coating, so that the animal
depends from this trumpet as from a buoy. Along the
sides of the otherwise naked body, there is a row of
stiff, thick bristles that ventrally form a kind of groove
within which the anterior appendages, likewise covered
with combs of stiff bristles, carry out rowing motions.
The whole arrangement works like the filtering apparatus
of a *Daphina* (=water flea), and with its oral proboscis
the *Rhinostentor* removes from this filtration device the
planktonic organisms that are wafted in and caught
there.

In *Rhinostentor spumonasus* (the Frothing Trumpet

Snouter) the same relationships prevail, with the exception that the creature hangs not from its nasal trumpet but instead from a bubbly mass floated off from the latter; into this mass the Snouter withdraws for sleeping, for mating, and at signs of danger.

A visitor to the archipelago is provided with a very impressive experience by the foam floats of *Rhinostentor foetidus* (the Stinking Trumpet Snouter; Fig. 6), not only because they often float about in great masses on the most varied bodies of fresh water but because at times their unbearable odor ruins a sojourn at many of these otherwise so idyllic spots. *R. foetidus* lives alto-

[Fig. 6] Rhinostentor foetidus. (Orig.)

gether within these rafts that it has made. Its ventral collecting apparatus is reduced to a pair of small rakes with which the creature, creeping in regular paths about its raft and pulling itself along by the somewhat reduced nasal trumpet, gathers its food. This food consists of larval fungus gnats of the genus *Spumalgophilus,* that browse on the mycelia that ramify throughout the floating mucus. The fungus, that has not been positively identified although it is one of the Eumycetes, is nourished by the dying blue-green algae that swarm throughout the floating mucus. Thus there is a symbiotic system: *Rhinostentor,* via the nutrients contained in the mucus and excreted in the urine and feces, supplies the algae with a suitable substrate, that is enclosed by the fungal strands. The algae assimilate this food and are then partly sucked dry or metabolized by the fungus.* The fungus is eaten by the larval fungus gnats. A part of these larvae furnish the rhinostentorian's food.

It is of interest that the mucoid rafts of *Rhinostentor spumonasus* and *Rh. foetidus* are inhabited by a whole series of other animals: Fritsch's Megaphone Bird regularly makes use of them as a nesting site. The six-winged damselfly, *Hexapteryx handlirschii,* deposits its eggs on them; and the larvae that hatch eat the larval fungus gnats. A whole series of Springtails (Collembola), among many other creatures, lives in the oxygen-rich air bubbles on the upper surface of the floats.

* Whether this constitutes a modified lichenaceous symbiosis is uncertain.

SUBTRIBE: Georrhinida (Burrowing Snouters),
FAMILY: Rhinotalpidae (Mole-like Snouters),
GENUS: *Rhinotalpa* (Mole Snouters),
4 Species,

GENUS: *Enterorrhinus* (Gut Snouters),
5 Species,

FAMILY: Holorrhinidae (Allsnouters),
GENUS: Holorrhinus (Wholesnouters),
18 Species,

GENUS: *Remanonasus*[27] (Dwarfsnouters),
1 Species.

Although the Burrowing Snouters have a thoroughly primitive-looking *nasarium*, that doubtless has been derived from that of the ancestral Snouters, nevertheless they are remarkable in that in extreme cases the snout predominates heavily over the rest of the entire body. In this respect—quite apart from the concomitant reduction of their whole structural organization—they are unique, not only among Snouters but among all vertebrates.

Relationships closest to those that originally prevailed are shown by the genus *Rhinotalpa* (Mole Snouters); and from these we choose as a typical representative

---

[27] *remanere* Lat.=to remain; *nasus* cf. Footnote 1.

[Fig. 7] Rhinotalpa phallonasus. (Orig.)

Rhinotalpa phallonasus, the Glansnosed Mole Snouter, which is native to Mairúvili (cf. Fig. 7). This is a creature the size of a mouse and has more or less the habits of a mole; i.e. it lives in passageways it has dug in the humid ground and feeds on soil insects and earthworms. Both fore- and hind-appendages are greatly reduced. The *autopodium* is very well preserved and together with the large claws serves both as a pushing device and as an anchor in the tunnel. The labor of digging, however, is carried out by the snout, that is equipped with large erectile organs and into which spacious air sacs (derived from the nasal sinuses) are incorporated; these last also contribute to the expansion of the snout. Not only around the thickest portion of the snout but also around the occiput and ventral to the lower jaws are wreaths of strong, posteriorly directed bristles; both wreaths can be extended and are concerned in locomotion, that occurs in the following phases: 1. the wreath of bristles on the throat is spread out, as are the claws of the appendages; 2. the snout is inflated by taking air in through the mouth and simultaneously closing the glottis (contributory is the ability to close off the *nares*); 3. the nasal wreath is extended; the air is blown out of the snout and the animal pulled ahead by contraction of *M. retractor nasarii,* after which Phase 1 may be repeated. The nasal erectile organs come into action only in very hard ground and then have the special function of stiffening and expanding the anterior end of the snout. But in general the animal does as little digging as possible and uses passageways that are already at hand; as a result of the way in which they were excavated they are very firm-walled. Along them the animal glides with remarkable speed, in the process gathering up, with a rake formed by the *chaetae submentales*,[28] the earthworms found on the way; it then removes the worms from the rake with the oral proboscis. The *papillae basonasales* play an important part in the perception of the prey. Their innervation, apart from that from the sensory facial nerves, comes also from those nerves that in related forms supply Jacobson's organ, and hence the *papillae* are organs both of the chemical and of the contact-olfactory sense.

At the posterior end, *Rhinotalpa* possesses above the tail a gland that serves for defense; this is especially important to the little creature because it is not able to turn around and because its tunnels frequently are inhabited by a small, aggressive species of land crab (*Chelygnathomachus*[29] *altevogtii*). Between the rudimentary hindlegs are also the teats; the young are pushed back to them briefly after birth. In this particular, *Rhinotalpus* displays signs of primitiveness, inasmuch as other monorrhines no longer suckle their young.

Even in *Rhinotalpa* there is already indicated a structural peculiarity that has been realized to a far greater extent in other representatives of the georrhinids: a

---

[28] An attempt has been made to trace the *chaetae submentales* back to the collecting basket of the rhinostentorids, and thus to derive the georrhinids from the hypogeonasids (Naquedai 1948). However, everything else in the organization of the two subtribes speaks against this conception.

[29] *chele* cf. Footnote 25; *gnathos* Grk.=dentition; *machómenos* or -*máchos* Grk.=a warrior.

tendency for filling the body cavity with connective tissue. In *Rhinotalpa* this holds only for the pleural regions, so that here the lungs are connected firmly with the pleural wall. In *Rhinotalpa phallonasus* this is less the case than in the smaller, closely related *R. angustinasus* (the Narrow-nosed Mole Snouter), in which are to be found yet other structural features that are unknown elsewhere among mammals and that are connected with the small absolute size of the creatures (cf. Fig. 8). Among these the following peculiarities should be stressed: reduction of the relative length of the digestive tract; decrease in pulmonary capacity; disappearance of the *nares;* lack of hair; expansion of the ciliated epithelium, that in *Rh. phallonasus* clothes only the larger sinuses, so that here it reaches the basal external region of the snout; simplification of the brain; reduction of the eyes; and finally, as the most striking physiological characteristic, complete loss of homoiothermy. Naturally all these structural and functional peculiarities are connected closely with the animal's habits; it does not live in solid ground, but in cavities in beds of coarse gravel. Therein it goes back and forth much like *Rh. phallonasus,* but with the difference that, in correlation with its longish build it is able also to undulate to some extent. Significantly too, the creature does not seek out only clefts that contain air but also those that are filled with ground water. In them it takes water into the lungs, that are reduced to simple sacs. The sinuses serve as additional respiratory organs. During rapid progression they too are filled rhythmically with water. When the animal is at rest, surface respiration through the richly glandular epidermis appears to suffice.

Developments already indicated in the genus *Rhino-*

talpa are much more fully emphasized in *Enterorrhinus,* the Gut Snouter. Representatives of this genus grow to a maximal length of 0.7 inches and display extraordinarily extensive reduction: of the extremities only the claws are retained, and their musculature can no longer be homologized with definite limb muscles. The gut is linear. Lungs are lacking. The heart is a simple circulatory tube, and its condition corresponds to that displayed elsewhere by young mammalian embryos. The entire body surface is ciliated. The brain completely lacks subdivisions, at least outwardly. Of the skeleton, only a weakly developed notochord can be distinguished; this extends dorsal to the gut and forward beneath the brain into the snout. As to the sexual organs nothing is known. The kidneys are protonephridia, with a single ciliated funnel on each side. This funnel sticks out into an endothelial sac, that lies at the base of the snout within the body cavity, which is filled with connective tissue. A genitourinary sinus no longer is present.

The genus is represented by a single species on each of the five big islands of the archipelago. There the animals live on the gravelly beaches of the deltas of small streams in a restricted region that is limited narrowly by the salt content of the ground water (ca. 0.6%–1.4%). Within such areas one often comes upon isolated snouts and upon specimens that, in relation to their body size, have either an extraordinarily large or exceptionally small snout, so that one is led to suspect that multiplication takes place by fission at the base of the snout.

Were it not that the Mole-like Snouters were already known and the relationship between *Rhinotalpa* and *Enterorrhinus* beyond question, never would one have suspected that the animals now grouped together in the family Holorrhinidae (Allsnouters) are Snouters. For these are tiny organisms, a few millimeters in size, whose structure has become so "primitive" that the thought of classifying them among the chordates would never have occurred.

In the first holorrhine genus, *Holorrhinus* (Wholesnouters), chordate structure has been retained in the following particulars: a slender notochord extends the whole length of the snout and through the entire, greatly reduced trunk. Present is a closed though reduced circulatory system that, however, bears early embryonic traits. Of the kidneys there is still on each side the ciliated funnel mentioned above; it opens into an endothelial *ampulla*. So far as sexual organs have been found—as yet only in the male—they lie not far from the rear of the animal, in a region where a band of well-differentiated muscle indicates the former position of the posterior limbs, that otherwise are no longer demonstrable. The musculature is inserted on bluntly protruding body angles, that play some part in digging activity. On the other hand, a whole series of structural features give the organisms a stamp divergent from that of the chordates: the lengthy nasal sinuses participate in digestion, in addition to the short, straight gut. They function as appendices or in a manner similar to that of the endodermal caeca of many investebrates, and are alternately filled with or emptied of food. The somatic muscles no longer are striated, but smooth. The brain is markedly reduced, and during early developmental stages the nerve tube becomes split into two strands of tissue from which there develop, adjacent to the notochord, two chains of ganglia that are connected by cross-commissures. The body cavity is filled with connective tissue. The outer surface, as is already the case in

Enterorrhinus, is covered with a ciliated epithelium, within which are scattered mucous cells that likewise have originated from the nasal passages. Additionally it is noteworthy that in the endothelial spaces of the adrenals rows of ciliated cells bear greatly elongated cilia, producing an effect like that of flame cells.

The 18 species of the genus *Holorrhinus* are distributed over the entire archipelago, living there partly in the sands of the flood plains and partly in the brackish waters of the coastal beaches. Locomotion normally is caudad. Two species (*Holorrhinus variegatus*=the Variable Wholesnouter and *H. rhinenterus*=Pinnochio's Wholesnouter) live in streams; frequently they have been reared successfully from apparently freshly deposited young, found as neurulae in an epithelial bladder, and this has provided interesting information about the structure of these animals. Thus, in the course of this work it has been shown that the eyes (these animals are able to see) arise as evaginations of the sac-like brain, but then persist as simple vesicular eyes while the brain is secondarily losing its central cavity and is becoming a broad, buckle-shaped structure the main ganglionic masses of which are disposed to right and left of the esophagus.

Up till now only a singe species of the genus *Remanonasus*[30] has been found, from the river sands of the Wisi-Wisi, a stream on Mairúvili island. This is a worm-like creature that reaches a maximal length of 2 mm. What distinguishes *Remanonasus menorrhinus,*[31] the Turbellarian-like Dwarfsnouter, from the preceding genus, is above all the loss of the anus and of the

[30] cf. Footnote 27.
[31] *menein* Grk.=to remain; *rhis* cf. Footnote 4.

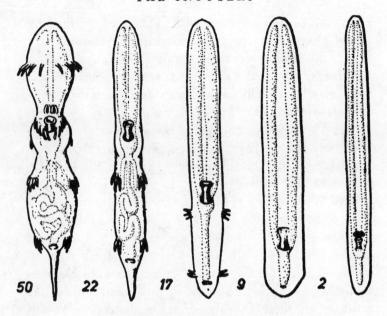

[Fig. 8] The anatomical series: *Rhinotalpa phallonasus—Rhinotalpa angustinasus—Enterorrhinus dubius—Holorrhinus ammophilus—Remanonasus menorrhinus.* The numbers show the over-all length in mm. Of the internal organs only the digestive tract is outlined. (After Mayer-Meier 1949)

system of blood vessels. Likewise there is no longer a trace of a notochord to be found. Unfortunately only males of these animals have been discovered up to the present. The kidneys no longer have any demonstrable ciliated funnel-like formation, but appear to be constructed like protonephridia, with a single huge cilia-bearing flame cell on each side.

Hence it is not surprising that various scientists have concluded that these animals are not to be counted among the Rhinogradentia at all. Müller-Girmadingen (1948) described them as *Dendrocoelopsis minutissima* and sought to classify them as Tricladida; however, Mayer-Meier (1949) showed with the help of careful histological investigations that particularly the mucus cells could not be looked on as typically tricladid. Nevertheless he was forced to grant that certain structural characteristics bore such great similarity to those of the tricladid Turbellaria that at least it was not altogether impossible that the tricladids had been derived from *Remanonasus*-like forms. Thus, the seemingly cephalic position of the testicles in the tricladids—that initially strikes any unbiased observer as odd—is comprehensible without difficulty when one recalls that the holorrhinids crawl backwards and that hence their caudal pole has become physiologically the anterior one. Furthermore, the form of the digestive tract first becomes completely understandable when—as illustrated by the transitional forms of the morphological series (cf. Fig. 8)—one derives it from the gut+nasal sinuses of the georrhinids. Of course the entire question can only be settled finally after animals with mature female sexual apparatus have been found. That this apparatus is so complex in the tricladids and in the turbellarians generally does of course suggest their derivation from more highly differentiated animals. Remane (1954) too emphasizes this, but would prefer to derive the Turbellaria from annelids. Stultén (1955) more recently is inclined to the opinion that the Rhabdocoela might have descended from annelids, but that the Tricladida (and the Polycladida, that in any case are to be derived from the latter) possessed rhinogradentiate ancestors.[31a]

31a For the sake of objectivity, it should be noted that Grassé, in his foreword to *Anatomie et biologie des Rhinogrades* (Masson & Cie, Paris 1962), contests that *Remanonasus* is a snouter. He prefers to take it as an endopsammic flatworm rather than a degraded Rhinograde.

The tribe of the sclerorrhines (the Proboscipedes) constitutes a series of the strangest and most beautiful species of the Rhinogradentia. Common to them is the fact that the *nasarium*[32] has become a leaping organ, a nasal leg, with which the animal can make mighty jumps; however, in view of the gravitational relationships (cf. Plate V), these are directed backward.

The most primitive conditions are found among the Arboreal Snout Leapers, the perihopsids,[33] whose appendages still bear a certain resemblance to those of the Archirrhiniformes. However, locomotorily to be regarded as the most typical are the Hopsorrhinidae, the Snout Leapers *sens. strict.*, in which the hind legs have disappeared except for slight remnants of the femur and tibia, and whose snout serves as the sole organ of progression. Finally, in the Orchidiopsidae (Orchidsnouterlike Snouters) the snout has become softened secondarily, in correlation with their more sessile habits.

[32] cf. Footnote 5.
[33] *peri* Grk.=around; *hopsos* cf. Footnote 4.

SUBTRIBE: Hopsorrhinida (Snout Leapers *sens. lat.*),
FAMILY: Amphihopsidae
(Two-way Snout Leapers or Arboreal Snout Leapers),
GENUS: *Phyllohopla* (Leaf Leapers),
2 Species,

FAMILY: Hopsorrhinidae (Snout Leapers
sens. strict.),
GENUS: *Hopsorrhinus* (Toothed Snout Leapers),
14 Species,

GENUS: *Mercatorrhinus* (Suctorial Snout Leapers),
11 Species,

Genus: *Otopteryx* (Earwings),
1 Species,

FAMILY: Orchidiopsidae
(Orchidsnouter-like Snouters),
GENUS: *Orchidiopsis* (Orchidsnouters),
5 Species,

GENUS: *Liliopsis* (Lilysnouters),
3 Species.

The Two-way Snout Leapers are creatures of the virgin forest and live in the crowns of the trees, where they leap nimbly from branch to branch or creep at leisure along the twigs. They are compactly built, and

33

like most Rhinogradentia are insectivores about the size of a mouse.

Whereas their torso and limbs have retained many archirrhiniform features, immediately conspicuous on the large head with its great eyes is the jointed snout, which ends distally in a dorsally located sole-plate and which is moved by powerful facial muscles and by a strong protractor, *M. extensor nasipodii longus* (=*M. longissimus nasarii*). According to Stultén, *M. extensor nasipodii longus* has been derived from the anteriorly lengthened *M. longissimus dorsi* or *M. l. thoracis*, as is indicated by its innervation via thoracic spinal nerves (cf. also Fig. 11). Just as oddly shaped as the snout is the tail; it too is exceptionally muscular and powerful and bears a terminal sole-plate, the strong bristles of which permit the tail to be braced firmly against roughened areas of the substrate (Fig. 9). In addition to the metameric

[Fig. 9] Phyllohopla bambola. (Orig.)

caudal muscles, that as a primary character have always been retained among the Rhinogradentia—a primitive feature to which Trufagura (1948) and Izecha (1949) have already drawn attention—it is above all *M. iliocaudalis* that acts as an extensor of the tail. Now, by means of the snout and the tail the periopsids are able to leap with improbable celerity back and forth through the thicket of vines, now frontwards, now backwards, and then sidewise, so that they are very hard to catch. This agility of theirs is at first hard to comprehend, since they are practically without enemies. However, they live together in small groups, within which there is a perpetual rushing to and fro, a chasing and a fleeing, that no doubt has to do with contests over their pecking order, the sociological significance of which has not yet been fully explained. In addition, their skill is of course useful to the animals also in their gathering of nourishment; for they feed almost exclusively on flying insects, that are snatched in the course of a leap.

The Hopsorrhinidae, in contrast with the preceding group of Snouters, live on the ground. As already mentioned, their hindlimbs are vestigial and no longer visible externally. The snout is even further differentiated than in the Perihopsidae, in that it has undergone a division into three segments; next to the head (cf. Fig. 10) is the *nasur,* which is connected by a joint with the *nasibia,* to which the *rhinanges* finally are autonasally attached. Extension of the *nasur* and the *nasibia* is by means of two separate bellies of *M. extensor nasipodii,* while the *rhinanges* are moved by the facial musculature and *M. flexores longi* and *breves* of the *nasipodium* (that is by those both of the *zygonasium* and the *autonasium*), which also are derived from the facial musculature.

35

As a result of ankylosis of the vertebrae and because of ventral stiffening provided by the sternum and the *processus styliformis*[34] of the pubis, the torso is firmly encapsulated. The forelimbs are mobile grasping organs. The tail no longer subserves progression but is used for securing the food, that consists primarily of amphipods, isopods, and little hermit crabs from the high tide level. In consequence, the supporting caudal sole-plate has been modified to constitute a pair of grasping tongs, the claws of which have been formed from modified or fused hairs and in cross-section present a histological picture resembling that of rhinoceros horn tissue. With this tail the Snout Leapers are most adept at pulling their prey out of the narrowest clefts and hiding places. Their leaps, that at ordinary speeds of progression cover about one-and-a-half body lengths but when fleeing or pursuing a mate or rival may be ten times as great, regularly are rearward (cf. Plate VI). The jump can be guided to some extent by slight movements of the huge ears.

The Snout Leapers belong to the most frequently encountered Rhinogradentia. Everywhere on the shore they inhabit the stony coral patches, the sands of the flood plains, or the volcanic or sedimentary gravel beds. It seems that the stronger males maintain small harems and drive off weaker males. However, the differences between the sexes are so slight that field observation has not yet permitted analysis of details of behavior within the packs.

Stultén placed the first two genera of the Hopsor-

[34] The *p. styliformis* is a structural innovation, that has nothing to do with a *pro-* or an *epipubis* and that also shows no relationship to the *os marsupialis* of the monotremes or didelphids.

rhinidae under the single genus *Hopsorrhinus*. However, more recently Bromeante de Burlas has reached the conclusion that the genus *Mercatorrhinus*[35] definitely deserves separation: whereas the *Hopsorrhinus* species all feed in the manner described above and in this connection possess the original type of dentition (whence also the common name "Toothed Snout Leapers"), all *Mercatorrhinus* species no longer are able to ingest solid food and are fully dependent on the symbiotic relationship described above (p. 15) with the Pillar-nosed Snouters of the genus *Columnifax*. This is apparent not only in the oral formation—absence of teeth, reduction of *M. masseter* and *M. temporalis*—but also in the vestigial nature of the forelimbs. Together with these reductions the animals, in correlation with their symbiosis, have acquired some capacities that are lacking in the idiotrophic forms. Thus, they are able to squat on the tail, which they coil beneath them, and do so regularly whenever, after having handed over their prey, they sit down next to a *Columnifax* to await their nourishment. (For the collator [Steiner] of these notes, however, De Burlas' arguments do not carry full conviction. Therefore, following Stümpke's own example, the question of the genus *Mercatorrhinus* is left open.)

That all the Suctorial Snout Leapers can be cultured readily was already noted at the beginning (p. xxiv), and depends on the ease with which artificial substitute food can be obtained: inasmuch as *Columnifax* milk is relatively rich in sugar and low in fat content and thus greatly resembles human milk, the animals can without difficulty be fed on condensed milk used for babies. Yet this is carried out successfully only with the help of an

[35] cf. Footnote 17.

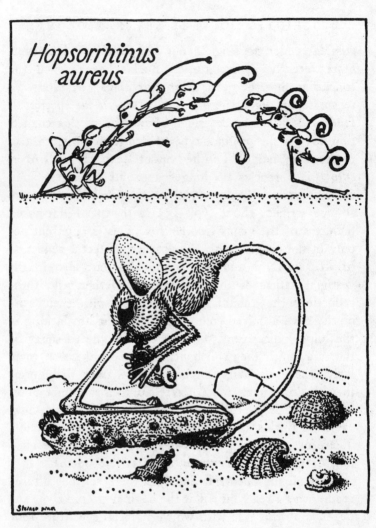

Hopsorrhinus aureus

PLATE VI

artifice that was discovered by exhaustive studies of the behavior of the animals:

When such a mercatorrhine is hungry, its drive to search for food is activated. The animal wanders about and sticks its tail into clefts and cracks in order to seize the aforementioned crabs. If it has taken prey, it then cautiously approaches a Pillar-nosed Snouter, and with characteristic leaps calls itself to the latter's attention. Not until a nearby *Columnifax* utters a grunt does the mercatorrhine come closer, and in fact approaches from the ventral side of the *Columnifax*. For its part, the latter keeps twisting constantly about its long axis at the approach of any animal whatever, always ready to squirt the secretion of its stink glands toward the potential attacker. But now *Mercatorrhinus* comes nearer in such a way that it makes repeated sidewise leaps to left and right, so that *Columnifax* can see it clearly. At intervals too it stands on its snout and with the tail holds aloft the prey, which it waves vigorously and vibrantly from side to side. Only when *Columnifax* ceases its lengthwise writhing and lets a long, guttural snuffling be heard, does *Mercatorrhinus* close in from the ventral aspect and hand over its medium of barter, its prey. Thereupon *Columnifax* examines this, to see that it is thoroughly fresh. If it is not, the Pillar-nosed Snouter at once assumes a defensive stance and squirts stinking secretion all over the bearer, unless the latter has meanwhile leaped hastily away to a safe distance. Only when the "goods" are beyond reproach does *Columnifax* offer its breast to *Mercatorrhinus*, that then gives a little hop onto its coiled-up tail and begins to suck.

Now, with captured mercatorrhines it next became apparent that they could not be maintained without *Columnifax*. On the other hand, adequate prey was to be

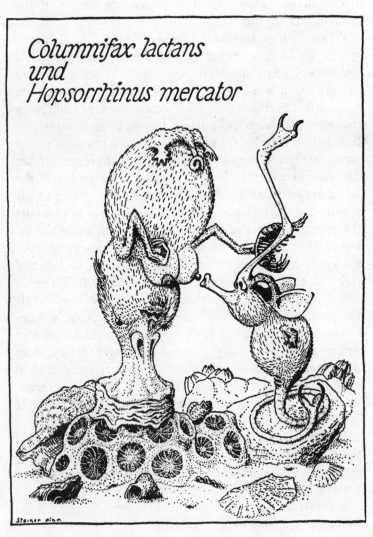

PLATE VII

gathered only with difficulty. But since incidental observations had shown that *Mercatorrhinus* did well on
the artificial diet mentioned, forced feeding was then
tried. However, this is tedious and often the very active
animals were injured fatally in the process. Only metic-
ulous observation of the rigidly determined "bargaining
rite" provided the solution: it was noted that *Mercatorrhinus*, even if it had found no food suitable for *Columnifax*, nevertheless would occasionally still attempt to
suckle. The above-mentioned "horrified" defense reaction of *Columnifax* fails to occur when *Columnifax* is
still sated from previous meals and also has an excess
supply of milk, the reduction of which has a pleasurable
aura. Under such circumstances the "deceitful" *Mercatorrhinus*, that for instance has proffered merely an
empty snail shell with no *Pagurus* inside, may be given
milk. On the other hand, *Mercatorrhinus* will not drink
without having first carried out the entire ritual of ex-
change. It has to have captured "prey" and have presented this, after having made the dancing approach
outlined above, before it will drink. Beyond this, the
following features on the part of *Columnifax* are essential: the shape of a wedge, thicker at the top; yellow
color; eye spots in the lower third; hissing sound; and
proper udder form. Besides it must take the "prey"
from the donor. One of Bitbrain's colleagues succeeded
in making a relatively simple electronically operated device that met the requirements indicated. At maximal
speed of operation it is able to suckle 80 *Mercatorrhinus* specimens an hour. Empty snail shells are used
as "prey"; after they have been accepted by the *Columnifax* model they gravitate beneath the false bottom
of the cage into cracks from which they can again be
fetched by *Mercatorrhinus*.

The peculiar *Mercatorrhinus*-fleas, that did great damage to the experiments in the beginning, can be controlled effectively by means of sticky paper on the underside of the upper layer of the double-bottomed cage (DDT and other insecticides are too toxic to *Mercatorrhinus*).

The Earwing, *Otopteryx volitans* B. d. B. (=*Hopsorrhinus viridiauratus*[36] STU.), the only representative of its genus, is by its structure readily to be recognized as a modified hopsorrhine (Plate VIII). Actually this animal is distinguished from its cousins only by the enormous size of the ears and the differentiation and strengthening, in correlation with its flight ability, of the musculature of the external ear. The one other difference, its vestigial tail, is a structural detail of little import. In all other respects, *Otopteryx* is a typical hopsorrhine, so that Stultén even hesitated to split it off from the other genera. However, in addition to what has been said, the following points are to be cited in favor of establishing a separate genus: the *nasarium* is extremely slender and gracefully constructed. The muscles that move the *rhinanges* are in part reduced, so that the animal is not able to run over uneven ground with the agility of the hopsorrhines. On the other hand, the abductors of the *rhinanges* are especially powerful; they serve to expand the *autonasium,* that functions as a steering tail. On the head there should be mentioned further the development of special bony ridges—the seats of attachment of the aural musculature—as well as the *os alae auris,* which however is not a bone but a calcified fibrous cartilage; and in addition the formation of air-filled lateral nasal sinuses beneath and within the bony ridges mentioned. In common with the hopsorrhines, *Otopteryx* displays

[36] *viridi-auratus* Lat.=greenish-gold.

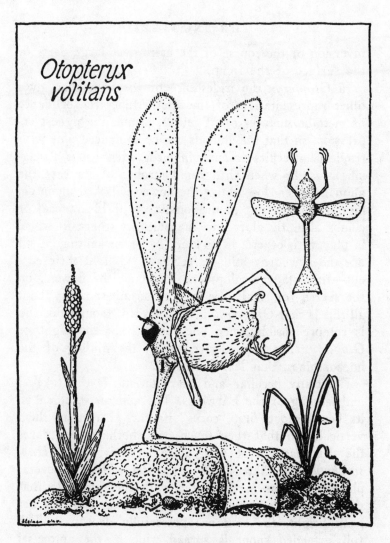

*Otopteryx
volitans*

PLATE VIII

inversion of the course of the hairs over large parts of the surface of the rump.

In *Otopteryx* the iridescence of the pelt, that gives other representatives of the sclerorrhines the brilliance of metallic surfaces or of jewels, attains its highest expression, so that the animals can be compared only with tropical butterflies or hummingbirds. Hence it is a magnificent sight when with rapid strokes of its ears the animal dashes close above the flower-bedecked mountain meadows in pursuit of dragonflies or of Hexaptera, or climbs abruptly aloft into the blue sky, there to wheel in play with others of its kind. Most enchanting of all are the newborn—still scarcely able to hold their ears out—that stagger calopteryx-like about the flowers, on the search for small insects. The strangest thing about all this is that *Otopteryx* flies backward, though this too is comprehensible when one recalls that the flight of *Otopteryx* has been derived from the gliding of the hopsorrhines, that leap backward.

Especially peculiar and characteristic is the take-off and landing of the Earwings. The animal, standing on its flexed snout, first "cocks" its ears, i.e. raises them vertically so that they touch one another; then flexes the deutonasal joint even more strongly, as in *Hopsorrhinus* (cf. Plate VI above); after which the several phases ensue as in the latter, with the difference that the leap is more vertical. Shortly before the jump reaches peak height, the ears are powerfully depressed. The fully-extended snout is spread wide in the autonasal region, and the animal flies. These individual phases can of course be analyzed only by high-speed photography. The process of flight itself is extremely rich in variety: when an adept insect is being pursued, or during playful flight maneuvers, great distances are traversed at blinding speed, with the ears beating uninterruptedly up and down at a rate of about ten strokes/sec. During searching flight, earbeats of equal frequency but of small amplitude alternate with short periods of gliding. Along the slopes, in the usually breezy island winds, *Otopteryx* also is able to soar at length. At all events it does not often go high into the air, and for the most part remains at altitudes not above twenty yards. Its method of landing is peculiar, being rendered difficult by the fact that the snout must perform in a double capacity, both as a foot and as a steering tail: if an Earwing wishes to come to earth, it mostly approaches the landing place in a steep glide, with the ears held somewhat dorsad and nasad. When close above the ground it suddenly adopts a vertical stance with the hind end somewhat elevated, which results in an abrupt, temporarily upward arc during which the steering tail—i.e. the tip of the snout— almost touches the earth. In this position, in which the ears are strongly arched (*M. inarcantes auris*[37]) the animal glides forward for yet a short stretch close above the ground, losing altitude and velocity the while. Then it suddenly folds the nasal steering mechanism together, curves the snout ventrad, and after elevating the ears to their full extent lets itself settle elastically onto the snout, which by now is stretched far caudad. This last phase of the alighting process again bears a great resemblance to the landing of the hopsorrhines after a leap (cf. Plate VI above, phases 6–8).

The way in which *Otopteryx* has solved the problem of locomotion—from the morphological standpoint a most extraordinary solution—calls for a comparison with the other flying forms of the animal kingdom. With

[37] *inarcare* Lat.=to arch.

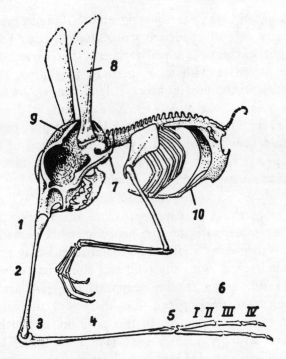

[Fig. 10] *Otopteryx volitans*, skeleton. 1. *Articulatio nasofrontalis;* 2. *Nasur;* 3. *Articulatio deutonasalis;* 4. *Nasibia;* 5. *Articulatio carponasalis;* 6. *Rhinanges* (=*Nasanges*) I–IV; 7. *Processus jugalauris;* 8. *Os alae auris* (=*Cartilago aeroplana*); 9. *Christa temporalis;* 10. *Processus pubici.* (Orig.)

exception of the Rhinogradentia themselves, true fliers have appeared only four times altogether: the insects, the flying reptiles, the birds, and the bats. Among these, the insects, whose organs of flight are supplementary additions not made at the expense of terrestrial locomotion, actually have found the most complete solution. The bipedal gait of birds likewise permitted great mobility both on the ground and in the air, even though in actuality the wings were "stolen" from the mechanism for progression on land. Among the flying reptiles and the bats the power of flight arose at the cost of locomotion on foot; and therefore the two groups were not and are not fully qualified to compete with the others just mentioned. But in *Otopteryx* now the situation is just as favorable as in insects, i.e. the ears are actually supplementary instruments of flight. Nonetheless, *Otop-*

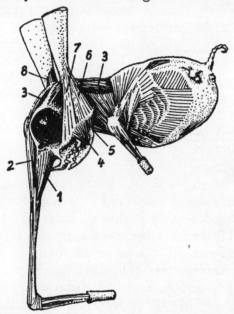

[Fig. 11] *Otopteryx volitans,* musculature.
1. *M. lacrymonasuralis;* 2. *M. extensor nasipodii superficialis;*
3. *M. extensor nasipodii longus;* 4. *M. masseter;*
5. *M. depressor mandibulae;* 6. *M. aeroplano-jugalauris posterior;* 7. *M. aeroplano-jugalauris anterior;* 8. *Levator aeroplanae.* To the right of 3, *M. extensor nasipodii* has been bared by partial removal of *M. trapezius cervicalis.* (Orig.)

teryx, with the high degree of limb reduction that pre-
ceded flight, has been derived from animals that were
strongly specialized in a single direction—yet in their
nasal "monopody" they are quite comparable to hopping
birds. In any case *Otopteryx* enjoys a clear advantage
over flying reptiles or bats; for it is a most skillful
leaper, and the participation of the snout in flight has
not limited its usefulness for terrestrial progression to
the same extent as has occurred with the anterior limbs
of these other groups. Whether *Otopteryx* could hold its
own in sharper competition with continental animals is
questionable. At all events it has scarcely any enemies
in the islands. Neither the indigenous Megaphone Birds
nor the seabirds, that are numerous from time to time
along the coast, can catch it in flight. In agreement with
this is the fact that one rarely finds pregnant specimens.
The period of gestation is at least as short as with
the hopsorrhines. Only a single foetus is carried at a
time (Harrokerria and Irri-Egingarri). It is suspected
that the females bear two young per annum.

The Earwings are not to be kept in captivity, because
they remain too easily frightened, bruise the buttocks in
their wild leaps and attempts at flight, and soon succumb
to the infections that arise in the wounds.

The Orchidsnouters (Orchidiopsidae) can be traced
back to hopsorrhine ancestors that exchanged the terrestrial way of life for an arboreal one, but that already
possessed the various hopsorrhine reductions—in particular the disappearance of the hindlimbs. Hence, adept
climbers could no longer be developed from them. Instead there must have been initiated an evolutionary
course in which the animals no longer leaped from place
to place but rather climbed slowly about with the help
of the forelimbs and the tail. Representatives with a

functional nasal leg are at all events no longer known, and in their habits and construction the *Orchidiopsis* and *Liliopsis* species of today are so highly specialized that initially their derivation from Snout Leapers was not even considered (cf. Gaukari-Sudur, Bouffon and Paigniopoulos). However, in the meantime some developmental data of evolutionary significance have been gathered, and from them it is clear, without possibility of contradiction, that a *nasur* and a *nasibia* as well as rhinanges are at first laid down in the embryonic *Orchidiopsis* snout but are later resorbed, so that the snout of the fully developed animal must be regarded as having been softened secondarily. (Bouffon and Zapartegingarri 1953 write: *"Les embryons des Orchidiopsides ne manquent point ni de nasur ni de nasibie, mais pendant le développement [longueur de l'embryon environ 15 à 18 mm] il y a lieu un ramollissement progressif de ceux-ci, de telle façon, que le nouveau-né ne montre plus aucune trace d'ossification dans son nasarium aplati et pétaloïde."** *) It is especially to Bouffon and his school that we are indebted for the further explanation of the organizational peculiarities of the Orchidiopsidae. Thus Bouffon and Lo-Ibilatze-Sudur were able to show that the secretory attractant (*"mucus attirant"*) of the *Orchidiopsis* species is not formed by the outer nasal surface, which in fact lacks any glandular cells that could be thus involved. Rather, it is produced by the great glandular fields of the inner surface, along the nasal passages, and is thereafter spread manually over the outer surface of

---

* Translation: (Bouffon and Zapartegingarri 1953 write: "Embryonic orchidiopsids lack neither a *nasur* nor a *nasibia*, but during development [length of the embryo from 15 to 18 mm] these undergo a progressive softening such that the new-born animal no longer shows any trace of ossification in its flattened, petal-like nasarium.")

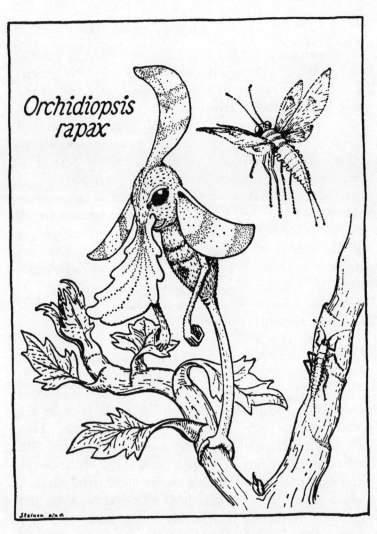

Orchidiopsis rapax

PLATE IX

the snout. Furthermore, the same authors succeeded in demonstrating that the grasping mechanisms of the tail are homologous structures in *Orchidiopsis* and in *Hopsorrhinus*. And finally Asteiides, a pupil of Bouffon's, was able to bring proof that in the snout of orchidiopsids there are vestiges of *M. extensor nasipodii,* that during embryonic development have the location characteristic of the hopsorrhine Rhinogradentia.

Ankel's Vanilla-perfumed Orchidsnouter, *Orchidiopsis rapax,*[38] the best-known representative of the family, lives in the forests of Mitadina, especially at the level of the higher tree crowns, but also at more moderate elevations where windfalls or floods have left openings in the woods (Plate IX). Ordinarily the animal stands motionless on its tail and hence, seen from afar, bears a certain resemblance to a big flower.[39] The genesis of the similarity is that the huge ears, the median dermal comb, and the flattened snout, protrude with vivid colors like floral petals from the head, whereas the inconspicuous green torso is at first inapparent. The already mentioned attractant secretion on the snout smells of vanilla and acts as an odorous lure. Insects that settle on the snout or that flutter close above it are snatched like lightning with the prehensile paws at the ends of the long, thin arms, and are conveyed to the mouth. Occasional changes of location are made with chameleon-like slowness, with the help of the forepaws and the two-clawed grasping tail. As to the mutual interrelationships among

[38] *rapax* Lat.=rapacious.

[39] Since orchids do not occur on any island in the archipelago, the name *"Orchidiopsis"* actually is an unfortunate choice; there is in fact no orchid-mimesis in the situation. At all events, these flowers (*Rochemontia renatellae* ST.) that are the models for the mimesis of *Orchidiopsis* are superficially very similar both in appearance and odor to orchids, although they are closely related to the Ranunculaceae.

the several individuals of a species nothing is known; however, about a dozen pregnant specimens carrying embryos in various stages of development have been taken up to now (cf. above).

Among the three *Liliopsis* species, that are distinguished from *Orchidiopsis* by the position of the ears and the cephalic combs, there is one that sleeps by day and "blooms," i.e. maintains its predacious pose, at night. This animal, commonly called the "glowing lily" in English and the *"Wundernase"* (=Miracle Snouter) in German (*Liliopsis thaumatonasus*), is extraordinary in that its mucous attractant gives off light. As with the luminescent slime of other animals (cf. Buchner), in the "glowing lily" too the light evidently is produced by symbiotic bacteria. At all events the tiny slime organisms that are held responsible have not yet been cultured, and electronmicrographic magnifications have failed to confirm their cellular nature beyond question.

SUBORDER: Polyrrhina (Multi-Snouters),
PHALANX: Brachyproata (Short-nosed Snouters),
TRIBE: Tetrarrhinida (Four-Snouters),
FAMILY: Nasobemidae (Snout Walkers *sens. lat.*),
GENUS: *Nasobema* (Snout Walkers),
5 Species,

GENUS: *Stella* (The Small Snout Walker),
1 Species,

FAMILY: Tyrannonasidae (Predacious Snouters
sens. lat.),
GENUS: *Tyrannonasus* (The Predacious Snouter),
1 Species.

As the name indicates, the Polyrrhina are set apart by the possession of several snouts. In this feature they exemplify a peculiarity that, though it appears as an element foreign to mammalian systematics, nevertheless —if considered generally—is repeated in other phylo-genetic series of animals, i.e. a multiplication of organs that in more or less closely related forms occur singly or in single pairs, or that are present in only a few of these related forms. As is well-known, one can—at least in thought—derive all the Articulata from polym-erous creatures whose counterparts or whose earlier ancestors are oligomerous; similarly there may be men-tioned here the variable number of gill slits among the relatively closely related lower vertebrates. Now, the multiplicity of the snout in the polyrrhine Rhinogradentia appears—purely formally—as the mere multiplication of an organ at an early embryonic stage (cf. Fig. 1). At all events it is not proper to cite it simply as an example of multiple malformation or mismodification and to draw a parallel between it and what is known from the morphogenesis of aberrant *Drosophila* mutants, as Knaddle and Kicherling have tried to do. Middlestead and Hassenstine very rightly have emphasized that with simple duplications the independent movement of the several snouts would necessarily be impossible, since one knows through the investigations of P. Weiss among others that such duplications receive identical motor impulses. Thus among the Rhinogradentia polyrrhiny is accompanied by a corresponding central nervous coordination of an equally great degree of differentiation. From the evolutionary standpoint this situation holds within it significant difficulties, when one recalls that the Rhinogradentia must have arisen at the earliest in the Upper Cretaceous. According to Remane (1954) it must be taken as an indication of relative primitiveness that among the polyrrhines there exist at least three groups with respect to the condition of polyrrhiny: those with four, those with six, and those with 38 snouts, quite apart from the various types of nasal differentiation within these groups. Also it is to be assumed that the separation of these groups took place very early; just as the separation of the polyrrhines from the monorrhines must have occurred very early. In the current state of investigation it is even difficult to trace the polyrrhines back to *Archirrhinos* or to archirrhiniform primitive Rhinogradentia. It is altogether erroneous to try to trace the polyrrhines back to nasestrian monorrhines, as d'Epp has attempted to do (Stultén 1949; Bromeante de Burlas 1949). One of the main reasons for this judgment is that the structure of the *nasarium*— quite apart from the matter of polyrrhiny—is altogether different, and that the reduction of the hindlimbs is accomplished in quite a different manner, moreover that the number of ribs and the development of the zygapophyses of the vertebrae in the monorrhines is completely aberrant (in the direction of the conditions seen in the Xenarthra, but of course as a manifestation of convergence), whereas the polyrrhines have more nearly maintained the original relationships.

Nevertheless the mono- and polyrrhines do exhibit one feature in common: the expanded tear duct, that in many instances serves as a respiratory passage. Bromeante de Burlas regards this as a result of structural convergence, that probably is related to the change in function of the snout(s) and their cavities. So it comes about that the distal nasal openings, in those forms where they occur, mostly subserve special functions that are not connected with respiration: olfactory examination, the intake of food, and finally even participation in the production of the animal's voice (cf. p. 83).

Details regarding the construction of the *nasarium* cannot be given in this concise report. For them we make reference to the studies by Bromeante de Burlas, Stultén, and Bouffon, as well as to the comprehensive exposition of these matters by H. Stümpke.

The Great Morgenstern's-Nasobame, the hónatata of the natives (*Nasobema lyricum;* Plate X), is the best-known representative of the polyrrhines and on this account will be discussed in somewhat more detail. As a typical polyrrhine it has on its short, fat head four equal snouts, that are fairly long and on which—as already

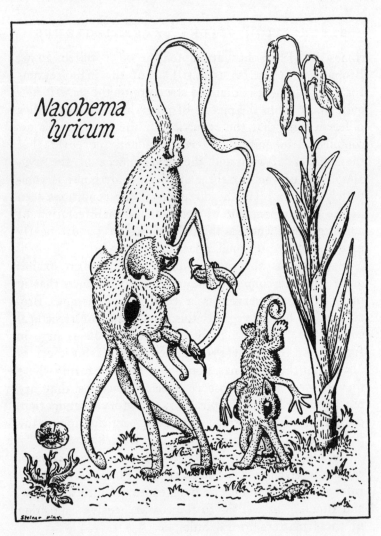

Nasobema lyricum

PLATE X

described by Morgenstern—it walks. It is enabled to do this, despite an inadequate nasal skeleton, because the snouts are rendered quite rigid by the strong turgor of their *corpora spongiosa*. Besides there ramify through the snouts highly branched air-passages, the filling of which is regulated by the *ampullae choanales* (differentiations of the soft palate at the margins of the *turbinalia*, that extend far ventro-caudad), so that the turgor of the snout is ensured by two systems: the hydraulic system of the *corpora spongiosa*, that is responsible primarily for the lasting rigidity required in walking, and the pneumatic system, that endows the gait and the movements with elasticity and that reduces the danger of damage when hard objects are encountered unexpectedly. In addition to the part played by the *ampullae choanales* a contribution is made by the *ampullae pneumonasales*, that are formed from the powerfully developed nasal sinuses. There are three of them on each side and they distribute the air delivered under pressure by the *ampullae choanales*. The *canales ramosi* of the snouts themselves have yet another *orificium externum* below the tip of the snout; mostly it is kept closed, but it can be opened reflexly very rapidly if strong mechanical stimuli impinge on the snout, so that the latter can collapse instantaneously. The system mentioned is innervated from *N. trigeminus*, while *N. facialis* supplies primarily the perinasal circular and longitudinal musculature. Like all polyrrhines, *Nasobema* lacks the *os nasale* altogether; it is not even laid down in the embryo.

The paired appendages are relatively well-developed. Very young animals display but little reduction of them. With older specimens, i.e. with those that have attained about ⅔ of the maximal body length, the posterior limbs are practically immovable and are also without function. The forelimbs are prehensile organs that are supplemented effectively by the long, lasso-like tail.

The tail is specialized to an extreme degree, and its organization is to be understood only in relation to the habits of the Nasobames. It serves these fructivorous animals for fishing down their food from great heights. The way in which this is accomplished is that the tail, only the proximal portion of which is penetrated by the vertebral column, incorporates a gas-filled channel that is connected with the coecum; so that, after the *sphincter gaso-tubalis* has been relaxed, the canal can be filled suddenly with belly-gases, whereupon the tail is abruptly blown taut and hurled upward to a height of more than four yards. Because of a strongly musculated *ampulla* (cross-striated fibers, derived from the ilio-caudal musculature) at the base of the tail, this occurs with such violence that in the twinkling of an eye the tail is projected with a slight pop to its full length. No sooner has the tip of the tail, richly supplied with tactile papillae, seized the fruit than the gas is released with a gentle whistle from the tail, that again becomes a flattish ribbon and contracts. The fruit that has been pulled down is then seized by the forepaws and brought to the mouth. It is interesting that the production of gas in general is rather well adapted to this mechanism: the hungrier an animal is the more strongly inflated is its colon and hence the *ampulla gasomotorica*. Related is the fact that very hungry animals, even when no reward is in sight, will carry out a "dry run" of the fruit-catching performance or will hurl the tail aloft toward all sorts of objects that resemble fruits. This is especially noticeable with *Nasobema aeolus*[40] (The Bluenosed Nasobame).

[40] *Aeolus* Grk.=the wind god.

Once a year *Nasobema* bears a single young that at first is carried about in the throat-pouch, which opens caudad, and that nourishes itself from the mother's axillary teats. The throat-pouch occurs only in females and is supported by cartilages derived from those of the Adam's apple. The animals are monogamous and the two sexes are very tender toward one another. The *postpartum* female is fed by the male. Only on the largest islands of the archipelago do the Nasobames have enemies, in the predacious Nasobames (*Tyrannonasus imperator* B. d. B.=*Nasobema tyrannonasus* STU.) that occur there. It is remarkable that the Hooakha-Hutchi, at their equinoctial ceremonies that took place each fall and spring, ate Nasobames roasted in leaves at these ritual feasts. They regarded the animal as holy, and did not hunt it except in connection with these religious rites.

The genus *Stella* was erected by Bromeante. Stultén still assigns *Stella matutina*[41] B. d. B. to *Nasobema,* as *Nasobema morgensternii.* The differences between the two genera are indeed small, and have to do with the tail-hurling mechanism, that is considerably less highly differentiated in the Little Morgenstern's-Nasobame, a situation that no doubt is related to the fact that *Stella mautina* lives almost exclusively on berries that grow near the ground.

In contrast with the peaceable Nasobames, the only extant representative of the tyrannonasids is a predacious fellow that feeds almost exclusively upon them. In its organization, Heberer's Predatory Nasobame, *Tyrannonasus imperator* B. d. B. (=*Nasobema tyrannonasus* Stultén) indeed resembles the Nasobames in all major respects, but differs in the development of the tail, that—

[41] *stella matutina* Lat.=*Morgenstern* (=morning star).

as in the rhinocolumnids—bears a poison claw at the tip; and besides of course because of its predatory teeth, the sharp points of which are suited for ripping the flesh from the victim. Additionally remarkable is the fact that the posterior limbs are astonishingly well-developed for a nasestrian species, as is related to their employment in seizing the prey. Finally it may be mentioned that there is no grain to the coat of this species, whose pelt gives rather a plushy impression, somewhat like that of a mole.

Tyrannonasus imperator is especially noteworthy for two reasons: like all polyrrhine species the animal is not particularly swift on nose, and yet it travels at a more rapid pace than the nasobemids. But now, since all polyrrhine species, because of their intranasal pneumatic apparatus, when walking give out a whistling hiss that can be heard from afar, *Tyrannonasus* is unable to creep silently upon his victims; but—since they flee while he is still at a distance—must first lie quietly in wait and then stride after. In this process of flight and pursuit that, because of the considerable expenditure of noise and the yet so moderate velocity, at first strikes the onlooker as comical, *Tyrannonasus* often must trail the intended victim for hours in order to catch up with him, since *Nasobema* uses the tail in flight also, by hurling it aloft, encircling branches with it, and thus swinging across ditches or small streams. Even when the predator has come very near the object of his pursuit, *Nasobema* often also employs the tail successfully as a last resort; hanging by the tail from a branch, it swings back and forth in circles or with broad pendular movements close above the ground until the predator, in his constant efforts to grab the prey, finally gets dizzy and throws up.

Tyrannonasus imperator

PLATE XI

Then, during this interval of the predator's disorientation, *Nasobema* frequently is able to make off.

But once *Tyrannonasus* has actually taken hold of his victim, the latter has no further hope of escape: by means of the toxic claw he is poisoned and soon collapses in tears, while the predator gives him the *coup de grâce*, hauls him to a shady spot, and there at leisure devours him down to the larger bones. Whereas a most striking characteristic of *Tyrannonasus* thus is his tough endurance in pursuit, a second peculiarity is the additional ability to fast for an extraordinarily long time for a mammal. This capacity is related both to an astonishingly low basal metabolic rate and to the ability to store glycogen not only in the liver but in subepidermal depots. Histologically the latter are composed of derivatives of the same embryonic cells as those that give rise to the fatty tissue that occupies this location in other organisms. Storage of energy in the form of glycogen rather than fat seems to be more economical, at least in *Tyrannonasus*. As this process progresses after feeding, the engorged animal becomes quite misshapen in a couple of days; immediately after its ample repast it lies down in a spot protected from the rain and dozes there until the subepidermal store of glycogen is depleted, which takes several weeks. Only after the animal has grown slender again, but still retains in the liver sufficient reserves for possible predatory pursuits, does it again become active and go out on the hunt.

The noteworthy fact that the captured Nasobame weeps has psychological interest, for it presupposes that the animal possesses insight and the power of reflection. In view of the considerable volume and degree of differentiation of the brain, such a possibility is not excluded (cf. in this connection H. W. Gruhle 1947).

In their nutritional physiology, the tetrarrhines (Four-Snouters) fall entirely outside the framework of the order and in this respect surely are secondarily divergent forms. According to Bouffon (1953) matters here are as follows: the Rhinogradentia are primarily insectivorous in habit, and the generally small size of the animals is correlated with this. In instances where there has been a specialization of the habits and way of nourishment that distinguishes the animals from the typical insectivorous type, they nevertheless are to be derived from it: all the crab-eating hopsorrhines (Snout Leapers) and their milk-symbiotic forms are close to this insectivorous type, and likewise the hypogeonasids (Mud Snouters) and the georrhinids (Burrowing Snouters) can be derived therefrom. With the tetrarrhines, whose more primitive members are out-and-out fructivores, such a derivation seems more difficult, although for example the dentition fundamentally is wholly of the insectivorous kind. Above everything else, the digestive tract displays extensive specialization, not to mention the gas-producing coecum. But the main factor that distinguishes the tetrarrhines from most other Rhinogradentia is the considerable body size. The Nasobames get to be nearly 3 feet high! The derivation of the Predacious Nasobame, *Tyrannonasus*, at first appears easier, inasmuch as seemingly a simple increase in all dimensions would convert an insectivorous into a predacious type. But Bouffon, by means of penetrating studies, has shown that *Tyrannonasus* has descended from the fructivorous species. This is revealed primarily in the organization of the digestive tract and of the tail, which during puberty is still nasobematous. Bouffon believes that the modification into a predator—and in fact into a monophagous predator—came to pass via a predatory commensalism. Certain peculiarities in the behavior of the predator give further indications in this direction: namely, it greedily devours fruits thrown aside by the fleeing Nasobames, and only attacks the latter when it can fall upon them while they are eating fruit. In agreement with this is the fact that young *Tyrannonasus* specimens are not predacious but merely pounce upon the feeding Nasobames in order to snatch their fruits away, or to feed upon the remnants of their meals.

This phenomenon, as Bouffon too points out, is by no means unique in the world of animals; the transition from the insectivorous to the fructivorous habit has frequently been observed, thus for example among the thrush-like songbirds, in the insectivores themselves, as well as in the South American Chiroptera, prosimians and catarrhine monkeys.

TRIBE: Hexarrhinida (Six-Snouters *sens. lat.*),
FAMILY: Isorrhinidae (Equal-snouted Snouters),
GENUS: *Eledonopsis*[42] (Ribbon Snouters),
5 Species,

GENUS: *Hexanthus* (Six-flowered Snouters),
3 Species,

GENUS: *Cephalanthus*[43] (Flower-faced Snouters),
7 Species,

FAMILY: Anisorrhinidae* (Unequal-snouted Snouters),
GENUS: *Mammontops*[44] (Shaggy-faced Snouters),
1 Species.

The tribe Hexarrhinida (Six-Snouters *sens. lat.*) comprises two very different families; whereas the Equal-snouted Snouters (Isorrhinidae) are small insectivorous animals of relatively primitive organization, the sole species in the family of Unequal-snouted Snouters (Anisorrhinidae) is of a type that at first glance seems much more reminiscent of the Nasobemidae but that also displays a whole series of features that separate it from

[42] *eledone* Grk.=an animal, related to the octopus.
[43] *kephalé* Grk.=a head; *anthos* Grk.=a flower.
* Translator's note *re* Anisorrhinidae: under most circumstances this should be Mammontopsidae, since *Mammontops* is the sole genus; however there are situations in which the rules of nomenclature would allow the family name Anisorrhinidae.
[44] cf. Footnote 15.

this family. Bouffon feels therefore that the tribe Hexarrhinida erected by Bromeante de Burlas cannot be upheld
or that it is polyphyletic. This will be considered later
when *Mammontops ursulus*[45] is discussed.

The Equal-snouted Snouters, as already said, are animals that—apart from their polyrrhiny—are to be regarded as primitive: the paired appendages are scarcely
reduced and still are well adapted for progression, even
though the animals make but little use of them. The differentiation of the snout likewise is still primitive.* On
the other hand, the progressive genera *Hexanthus* and
Cephalanthus Br. d. B. (=*Ranunculonasus* and *Corbulonasus* STU.) are distinguished by highly developed
mimesis, that has modified the exterior of the animals in
a most peculiar fashion. [Translator's note: Br. d. B. is
just B. d. B. elsewhere.]

As representative of the more primitive genus *Eledonopsis, Eledonopsis terebellum* (The Tubeworm-snouted
Ribbon Snouter) will be described:

In little holes in the ground, beneath stones and roots,
on Mairúvili one frequently finds a small animal the size
of a shrew, that sleeps there rolled up during the daytime
and on first glance looks just like a little shrew, with
grayish-brown fur and rosy paws. The little creature does
not try to run away and lets itself be put back into its
den. If one marks the position of such a hole and at night
makes a flash-photograph of its entrance and the surroundings, then one sees on the picture that four to six
ribbon-like structures are stretched forth from the hole.
These rose-colored ribbons are some 2–3 mm wide and
as much as a foot long. On the upper surface they bear

[45] *ursulus* Lat.=a little bear.
* but cf. page 76.

two narrow, damply glistening grooves to which are stuck, one sees, some tiny insects, mostly podurids (springtails) and barklice (Corrodentia). If one tries to view these structures more closely with a flashlight they are then pulled quickly back into the hole. For a long time the phenomenon failed to yield to more precise observation. In fixed specimens the ribbons were indeed to be identified without further ado as snouts, but their function became explicable only when the animals were kept permanently in the light (Schaller's method). Now it became apparent that the ribbons actually are the snouts, and the two grooves the drawn-out *nares* that have been swiveled upward; furthermore it was found that the ciliated epithelium of the nasal cavities was continued throughout the *nares* and that, together with the nasal mucus, served to transport the small insects that stuck there; these were swept into the nasal passages and were carried choanally to the digestive tract. Besides, it developed that *Eledonopsis* also is able to entrap larger insects—up to the size of woodlice—and move them proximad in this fashion, while the ribbon-like snout contracts and forms a gutter within which the prey is brought to the base of the snout, partly by means of the current set up by the cilia and partly by means of peristaltic movements of the trough. There the prey either is seized with the tongue or dug with the hands out of the nasal parts directed toward the head, and devoured. Interesting too is it that large, unwieldy animals—primarily spiders of the families Heieiatypidae and Lycosodromidae—are first entrapped in the nasal slime and then entwined by several snouts and drawn toward the head. As to when the various prey-catching mechanisms are set in motion, the decision is made in part by the very acute tactile sense and then too by the chemical sense, that

Eledonopsis suavis

PLATE XII

extends clear to the tips of the snouts. (Here it is a matter of receptors and nerves that bear the same relationship to the actual olfactory organ as Jacobson's organ in many other vertebrates.)

In *Eledonopsis* care of the brood differs in no wise from that of other Placentalia. A marsupial pouch is not present. The young become independent at a very early age. Mating seems to take place at night. Up till now attempts to rear *Eledonopsis* in captivity have been unsuccessful.

The behavior of young specimens of the Six-flowered Snouters (*Hexanthus*) is very similar to that of *Eledonopsis*. They too live in holes in the ground or under leaves and from there stretch out their snouts in order to catch prey. But this is true only of the very young animals that have just begun to get their own food after having been released from their mother's nursery. Later, the following differences from *Eledonopsis* come about: the nasal groove grows together, in a proximal to distal direction, in such a way that ultimately openings remain only at the base and the tip of the snout while the rest of the snout forms a covered tube. Then four broad, pointed dermal lobes grow out at the tip of each snout. According to the species, these are variously colored and are capable besides of fairly strong color changes within the limits set by the specific basic coloration.[46]

Eventually each snout comes to look like a long-stalked flower. During this modification of their snouts the animals scarcely change their habits at all. They continue to stretch their snouts forth from their hiding place, but

[46] Freddurista and Perischerzi have shown that reds are regulated by expansion of the capillaries, yellows by the superficial fatty tissue (that lies, however, below the subepithelial capillary net), and blues by black pigment situated in contractile melanophores.

curl them higher and higher about the stems of plants,[47] and get their nourishment as described above. At all events there now takes place a constantly greater change in the menu. For now they catch primarily flying insects that, deceived by the flower-like shape and color, settle at the tips of the snouts. Transportation of small victims continues in the manner already described. As also explained above, somewhat larger specimens are borne cephalad by peristaltic movements in the nasal tubes. Yet larger objects, that could not pass through, are—in contrast with *Eledonopsis*—not taken in entire. Instead, the very expansible, corolla-like flaps of the snout are folded about the insect so that it is practically wholly enwrapped; thereupon the *Hexanthus* vomits through the appropriate snout and digests the specimen to the point where it can be sucked back through the nasal tube.

Mature *Hexanthus* do not continue to lurk in holes; rather, they lie on rocky slopes amid the greenery of grassy patches and small herbs. Their own greenish coloration makes them inconspicuous there, and their snouts are for the most part twined about the stalks of those flowers whose color and shape they can simulate. Moreover, this adaptation contains a visual element: if *Hexanthus* is presented with blue flowers pasted to a sheet of cardboard behind which the snouts are lying among yellow flowers, then the rhinal corolla-like lobes turn blue —and vice versa. Furthermore, the various *Hexanthus* species have differing photoperiodic behavior; whereas the Globeflower Snouter (*Hexanthus ranunculonasus*= *Ranunculonasus pulcher*[48]) is thoroughly diurnal, the predominantly violet snouts of the Gorgeous Night-

[47] constantly to the left, both the snouts of the right side of the body as well as those of the left (cf. Ludwig 1932).
[48] *ranunculus* Lat.=a crowfoot (flower) ; *pulcher* Lat.=beautiful.

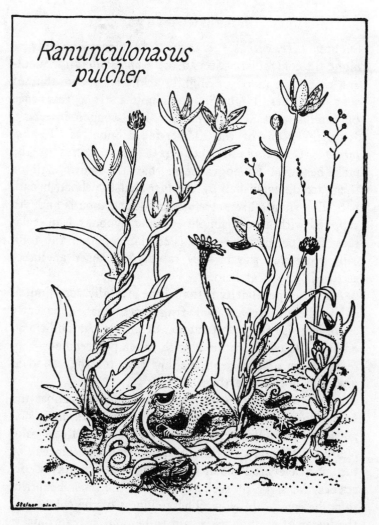

Ranunculonasus pulcher

PLATE XIII

Snouter (*Hexanthus regina-noctis*[49]) blossom mainly at night. In contradistinction to the *Ranunculonasus* Snouters, that have merely a slightly acidic odor, like that of sour milk, these Night Snouters emit a strong fragrance of vanilla, that attracts nocturnal six-winged insects.

To the genus of the Flower-faced Snouters (*Cephalanthus=Corbulonasus*) belongs a whole series of the most beautiful Rhinogradentia that are known. All of them are distinguished by the fact that the short, broad, petal-like snouts are set close about the mouth and are supplied with a very simple epi- and hyponasal musculature, that permits the animals to clap together the tonically outspread snouts very rapidly whenever an insect settles in the oral field.

A further peculiarity is that these mentally very limited animals emit strong oral fragrances, that apparently serve likewise for the attraction of insects. An additional oddity is that—in contrast with other polyrrhines—representatives of this genus neither care for the brood in any way nor suckle them.

As a typical representative of the genus we choose the Miraculous Flower-faced Snouter (*Cephalanthus thaumasios*[50]=*Corbulonasus longicauda*[51]), that lives colonially on Mitadina in the meadows of Ranunculaceae of the more elevated mountainous regions. Skämtkvist describes the sight of such colonies as the most beautiful thing he saw on Hi-yi-yi. The vividness of the colors and the luster of the snouts is said to be quite extraordinary, and the characteristic spectacle of the animals' swaying on their tails in the fresh sea breezes enchanting. Evidently what pleases us most in these curious creatures is

[49] *regina noctis* Lat.=queen of the night.
[50] *thaumásios* Grk.=marvelous, rare.
[51] *longi-cauda* Lat.=longtailed.

Corbulonasus longicauda

PLATE XIV

for the flower-seeking insects nothing more than the presentation of hypereffective stimuli: and in this sense too is to be interpreted the buttermilk-like odor that emanates from the open mouths of the lurking cephalanthids.

In addition to the *nasarium*, which has already been discussed, one of their striking features is the stiffened tail, that may be as much as twenty inches long. An interesting thing is how the caudal structure changes as the animal grows: the newly born animals, that already possess a fully developed *nasarium*, fall to the ground and climb up on the stems of nearby flowers. Having reached the top, they bite off all the buds, unfold the *nasarium*, and begin to capture prey just as older specimens do. Their still soft tail is then just about the length of the body and differs in no respect from a normal mammalian tail. But it promptly grows in length, and in fact by means of elongation of the vertebrae; as the intervertebral articulations ankylose and the intervertebral sinews and ligaments also stiffen, the caudal musculature degenerates, so that of *M. ischiocaudalis, M. iliocaudalis* and *M. depressor caudae* there remain only ligamentous bundles that are attached to the caudal vertebral column and to its rigidified uniting structures. The tip of the tail bears a much cornified epithelium, that eventually forms a sort of pointed, plugshaped horny cap. As soon as the tip of the tail reaches the ground, the animal that had climbed up the plant stem starts to bore this caudal plug into the ground, which within four to six days it penetrates to a depth of as much as 6 inches. Then the animal lets go of the plant stem and henceforth is supported by its own tail, that continues to lengthen. The degree of caudal extension attained depends on the nutritional state of the animal, and proceeds more slowly when the latter is well fed. An animal once firmly "planted" in this way can no longer move from its location, but simply waits there for prey with folded arms and open mouth. As mentioned, the mental capacities are slight. Mating takes place when it is windy: as the specimens are blown back and forth on their tails and come into contact, the desirous males take firm hold of the females. The period of gestation is said to be but three weeks, and the total duration of life is estimated maximally at eight months. Growth from birth to maturity requires perhaps two months; from birth to caudal implantation eighteen to twenty-two days.

Not infrequently one finds colonies that make a pitiful impression; the snouts look limp and are discolored and incrusted. The creatures are losing weight, and their soft whimpering is audible from afar. Such colonies have been attacked by a nasal scab, that is caused by a species of mite that is closely related to the gamasids. A slight infestation scarcely causes noticeable harm. But when mass increase of the mites renders the snouts ineffective for taking prey, this is naturally a catastrophe for *Cephalanthus*. The starving, tortured creatures then dig constantly at their diseased snouts and thereby merely increase their suffering. At the end there are only the little corpses hanging on their long caudal stalks; and in many places one finds standing in the meadows groups of sixty to a hundred skeletonized tails, beneath which there lie only the decaying remains of bones and hides. However, the primary cause of the epizoötics is not the endemic mites, but rather viral diseases favored by variations in the weather; they reduce the natural resistance to the mites, in that individuals suffering from viral disease are not able to give regular care to their snouts and to keep them properly lubricated.

The majority of *Cephalanthus* species live in the manner described. Only *Cephalanthus ineps*[52] (=*Corbulona-sus ineps*) and *Cephalanthus piger*[53] (=*Corbulonasus acaulis*[54]) have reduced tails and simply lie on their backs in sunny spots between stones and flowers. According to Bromeante de Burlas, their separation from other cephalanths as a new genus, already weighed above, does not seem justified.

As has been mentioned on p. 66, the anisorrhine *Mammontops ursulus* (The Bearlike Shaggyfaced Snouter), that likewise occurs in the mountain meadows of Mitadina, falls quite outside the hexarrhine series. It is a relatively majestic animal, that attains an over-all height of 4 feet 3 inches in the male and 3 feet 7 inches in the female; and is herbivorous.

Its snouts are differentiated somewhat in the tetrarrhine manner, and this is what causes uncertainty as to the proper systematic arrangement; whereas Stultén favors placing *Mammontops* in the immediate vicinity of the tetrarrhines, in that he lays more weight on the nasal structure than on the number of snouts, Bromeante de Burlas holds the opinion that the number of snouts deserves the greater systematic consideration, while the degree of nasal differentiation is to be regarded as due merely to convergence. In support of this view, he draws upon the investigations of the group of French scientists (Bouffon, Irri-Egingarri, and Chaiblin), who have shown that the innervation of the several groups of muscles in the tetrarrhines is quite different from that of *Mammontops*. Here it seems to be a matter of a further differentiation of the epi- and hyporrhinal muscle slips of the isorrhines; and the absence of *corpora spongiosa* from

[52] *ineps* Lat.=mentally sluggish.
[53] *piger* Lat.=lazy.
[54] *ákaulos* Grk.=stalkless.

Mamontops ursulus

Steiner pinx.

PLATE XV

the snouts of recent isorrhines no longer appears so primitive as was once assumed. Bouffon and Gaukari-Sudur postulate for the hexarrhines common tetrarrhine-like ancestors from which the isorrhines of today have developed on the one hand and the anisorrhines on the other. In this connection it is nevertheless a curious fact that the isorrhines display emphatically primitive features in respect to their paired appendages, while in the anisorrhinous line these are especially reduced. Moreover it is noteworthy that the hair whorls that are characteristic of the polyrrhines are lacking in the isorrhines. Against the placement of too much stress on this feature, Bromeante de Burlas brings up the point that even the surely secondarily evolved *Orchidiopsis* does not exhibit an inversion in the course of the hairs although such an inversion is most conspicuous in the much more primitive hopsorrhines. In any case the problem of the position of *Mammontops* will have to be left open for the present, until more extensive detailed investigations have been made.

Mammontops occurs in small herds that are led by older males. The animals feed almost exclusively on a composite, *Mammontopsisitos dauciradix,*[55] that they tear up by the roots with their two grasping snouts. The dentition is the most highly specialized known among the Rhinogradentia (aside from the total loss of teeth in the mercatorrhines): the incisors are reduced, the canines small and blunt, the premolars and molars broad and slab-like.

The Shaggyfaced Snouter suckles its offspring, that clings with its snouts to the thick fur of the mother and also to her stiff, inguinal teats. The reproductory rate is

---

[55] *sitos* Grk.=food; *dauci-radix* Lat.=a carrot-like root.

low. The animals seem to grow quite old. Older males are distinguished from the uniformly chocolate-brown younger males and the females by a silvery gray tail, the waving of which releases a following response on the part of the herd. For example, Tassino di Campotassi was able, by whitening the tail of a young female, to provoke a following reaction from the herd into which he put her. The whitened tail was particularly effective as a supernormal releaser of the following response in the younger males.

PHALANX: Dolichoproata (Long-nosed Snouters),
FAMILY: Rhinochilopidae[56] (Tasselsnouter-like
Snouters),
GENUS: *Rhinochilopus* (Tasselsnouters*),
2 Species.

The genus *Rhinochilopus* with its two species, *Rh. ingens*[57] (The Giant Tasselsnouter) and *Rh. musicus* (The Pipeorgan Tasselsnouter), possesses the most impressive polyrrhiny: in both these animals the head has been protracted into a long *proa* or rostrum. The underside of this structure is supported by the maxillary, the premaxillary and the palatine, the upperside by the maxillary, premaxillary and nasulary, as well as by a part of the nasal bone. The lower side (cf. Fig. 12) exhibits a lengthening of the oral cleft, the so-called proal groove (2), that is enclosed by the lips. At the anterior end of the *proa* the male bears two asymmetric incisors. To the right and left of this proal groove are the nineteen pairs of snouts, here termed *nasuli* (3, or 9). The first pair serves as tentacles, the rest as organs of locomotion.

[56] *chilo-pus* Grk.=a myriapod.
* Translator's note: "Tatzel" signifies "paw" rather than "tassel," but the English term "Tasselsnouters" seems more suitable for these animals.
[57] *ingens* Lat.=enormous.

(As to the more detailed structure of the *nasarium,* see below.) The paired appendages are much reduced. The hindlegs function solely as antennae for use during rearward movement. The forelegs do not touch the ground and also play no part in the uptake of food. In the female they serve to clasp the invariably single offspring. The tail too is no more than an organ of touch. The animals attain a respectable size (in *Rh. musicus* nearly 5 ft. from *proa* to the base of the tail, in *Rh. ingens* more than 7 ft.). They are omnivorous but prefer insects, snails, and fungi, and also berry-like fruits. Occasionally they also consume young leaves. *Rhinochilopus* is solitary, wandering in leisurely fashion through the virgin forest and especially through the less dense portions and the margins of the woods, where it has definite routes and stamping spots. However, the animals have no fixed beats, and make uncontested use of the paths of conspecific individuals.

The most noteworthy peculiarities of the two species, especially of *Rh. musicus,* are however the wooing procedure and the correlated nasarial specialization, that will be described briefly: like most Rhinogradentia, *Rhinochilopus* no longer respires exclusively through the nares, but predominantly through the tear duct, that likewise is expanded significantly, as it is in almost all species (cf. also Fig. 4). Now, on the one hand the tear duct (Fig. 12, 7) is connected immediately with the throat, from which a passage—the *ductus osmaticus*—runs into the *proa* and there gives off the *ductuli osmatici* (4) into the *nasuli.* On the other hand, the tear duct also is connected via the *ductus inflatorius* with the *vesica inflatrix organi* (8), which again for its part communicates by way of the *ductus vesico-gularis* with the throat. A second connection (6) between tear duct and *vesica inflatrix organi* and the *nasuli,* the *ductus musicus,* supplies the

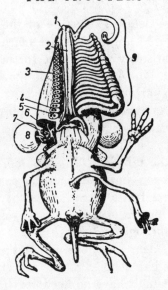

[Fig. 12] *Rhinochilopus musicus;* advanced embryo. 1. Incisor
rudiments (only in the male) ; 2. Subproal groove;
3. *Ductulus musicus* of one excised nasulus; 4. *Ductulus
osmaticus,* same; 5. Nasular *corpus spongiosum;* 6. *Ductus
musicus;* 7. Tear duct; 8. *Vesica inflatrix organi;* 9. *Nasuli.*
The more medially situated *ductus osmaticus* is not numbered.
Note the distinct structure of the first nasulus, apparent even
in the embryo. (After Bouffon and Gaukari-Sudur 1952)

ductuli musici, that are located in the *nasuli* laterad of the
ductuli osmatici. When at rest the *vesica inflatrix organi*
lies beneath the skin of the cheek, and on activation of
the nasal pipeorgan is inflated to the size of a child's
head. The apparatus as a whole constitutes a differentiation of the tear duct and the choanal portion of the
nose, as may be determined in young embryos. As additional components the pipeorgan includes the *corpora*

spongiosa (5) of the *nasuli,* as well as the nasular circular and longitudinal musculature.

In its entirety the apparatus operates as follows: during progression the *ductus musici* and *ductuli musici* are closed and together with the *corpora spongiosa* afford the *nasuli* the turgor required if the circular and longitudinal musculature is to suffice to move them. During inspiration, air flows in through the *ductuli osmatici.* Thus the air is constantly being tested. The first pair of *nasuli,* that function as tentacles, are especially concerned with olfactory examination. Directional olfactory testing is rendered possible by the division, in the *proa,* of the olfactory nerve in such a manner that each pair of *nasuli* comes to have a distinct olfactory epithelium. Food is taken in through the *nasuli* by being grasped by a digit-shaped lengthening of the nasular tip or by being encircled by the distal third of the entire *nasulus* and then brought into the proal groove. The prey is then impelled toward the mouth by the strongly protracted lips. The musical apparatus of the *nasarium* is made use of only during courtship. Then the males lie flat on the ground. The *ductuli osmatici* cease to function, as do the *corpora spongiosa.* Initially the nasalar musculature relaxes completely. Only the *sphincteres terminales* of the *ductuli musici* are slightly contracted. The *sphincteres glossiformes,* situated at the base of each *ductulus musicus,* are relaxed. Now, by means of violent, persistent breathing, the animal inflates the *vesicae inflatores organi* and thereby also puts the *ductus musici* under pressure. By opening slightly the *sphincteres glossiformes* the *nasuli* now are inflated, and though the circular musculature is fully relaxed the longitudinal musculature can make the *nasulus* longer or shorter. If now a *sphincter glossiformis* is suddenly opened more widely, brief puffs of air

pass into the corresponding *nasulus* and cause it to re-
verberate, inasmuch as the air column it contains is set
into vibration by the lips of the sphincter. Since each
nasulus can be lengthened or shortened in rapid alterna-
tion, it works like a wind instrument on the principle of
a slide trombone, with the peculiarity that long-lasting
tones cannot be produced, but only successions of short
ones. With eighteen pairs of *nasuli* that function in this
wise (the first pair lacks a *sphincter glossiformis*[58]),
the animal has command, so-to-speak, of 36 wind instruments that can be activated independently. How they are
employed in courtship has been described graphically by
Skämtkvist:

"At that time—it was the vernal equinox—the Hooakha-Hutchi were celebrating the hónatata feast, at which
the smoked hónatatas were consumed to the accompani-
ment of ritual chants in the village long house. It was in
the evening, at dusk. The ceremonial meal lasted not
more than two hours. Then the village company arose
and betook themselves to a nearby forest glade, at the
western edge of which they all sat down. The full moon
was already visible above the treetops on the mountain
opposite when the Móstada Dátsawima (the 'Lords of
the Myriapods') made their appearance from the dark
of the woods and stepped out into the glade. Silently, as
if they were floating, the great beasts moved. In the uncertain moonlight their legs (snouts) were not to be

[58] The *sphincter glossiformis* is not a simple circular muscle. The
entire closing mechanism summarized in the term is composed of the
actual sphincter, that extends around three-quarters of the circumference
of the *nasulus,* and a stout cushion of connective tissue, that occupies
the remaining quarter. On this cushion of connective tissue there sits
a V-shaped pair of outgrowths that act as vocal cords. The vocal apparatus might logically be called a "narynx," since it constitutes a
wholly comparable analog of the larynx and syrinx.

clearly made out. Only the luster of the long heads and backs could be discerned. There were fourteen or sixteen animals, that first paraded in a circle a couple of times before the six especially huge males lay down and extended all their snouts, while the females continued to circle about them. And now there began the most peculiar concert that I had ever heard: it began with the hollow, rhythmic lowing of one of the animals. Slow at first and then growing faster. Soon a second one joined in, lowing a few notes higher; and finally all six were taking part. The rhythm varied, but was maintained in rigid synchrony by all the animals, while the number of participating voices grew and grew. All at once there was a silence, and then a sharp, bleating tremolo, many-voiced and prestissimo, was superimposed on this rhythmic, half-rumbling, lowing or thrumming, hollow outcry. This constituted the second movement. In time, this 'solo' by the individual male concerned in its production was heightened by the weaving into it, in addition to the bleating and 'staccato' passages, of slurred and smudged tonal transitions. The beast that had the solo part could be distinguished by the fact that its snouts, that now were readily discerned inasmuch as they were extended to one side, were alternately inflated and made shorter and longer. Suddenly there was silence once again; and then the hollow basic pattern of the whole musical chorus started up once more, whereupon a second male gave solo voice. During this 'concerto' the females circled in slow, regular tempo about the performing males, until the last of these had finished his solo contribution. Then the males arose, and the whole ghostly company vanished slowly, as they had come, into the dark forest. The inhabitants of the village stood up, and bowed deeply toward the place into which the Móstada Dátsawima had disappeared, and deeply once again toward the full moon. Then we walked back into the village, where until the hour was late the pipes and drums resounded, a pale echo of the music heard earlier . . ."

Sad to relate, a thorough study of these animals was no longer possible, since they too—just like the Hooakha-Hutchi—soon fell victims to the head cold introduced by Skämtkvist. Skämtkvist did succeed, however, in capturing and taming one of the males. The animal seemed very intelligent, as is understandable in view of the weight of its brain, which was determined later. It grew very tame, and Skämtkvist was even able to teach it two of Bach's organ fugues that he knew by heart, so that it could perform them perfectly. Only its inability to produce long-held notes caused any difficulty. Here the animal made shift with very rapid tremoli, by using four *nasuli* adjusted to the same pitch.

EPILOGUE

HARALD STÜMPKE'S manuscript was awaiting publication when it became known that, during secret tests of atomic explosions (about which even the Press had heard nothing), the entire Hi-yi-yi Archipelago had been annihilated through the oversight of some subordinate. As a result of tectonic tensions that had not been anticipated, the whole group of islands sank beneath the sea when the burst was set off some 125 miles distant.

At the time in question, an international commission for study of the archipelago was in session on Mairúvili. Among those present were most of the scientists named in this work. With them there went down the Darwin Institute of Hi-yi-yi, situated on the lovely eastern bay of the islands, and in it the irreplaceable photographic material, the various preparations and observational and experimental records that were to have formed the nucleus of a great, comprehensive treatise concerning the archipelago and its geological, historical, zoological, and sociological peculiarities.

Thus it was most fortunate that, shortly before his voyage, Stümpke had undertaken to compose a short exposition of the structure and habits of the Rhinogradentia. Toward preparation of drawings he had supplied me also with some material that he—one can only say,

Alas!—took back to Hi-yi-yi with him. Still it was in this way that at least a part of the lifework of this modest and deserving seeker after Truth could be preserved as a balanced whole for science and for a broader audience, and with it the knowledge of a now-vanished world.

Heidelberg, October 1957   GEROLF STEINER

BIBLIOGRAPHY

ASTEIDES, S. (1954): Le nez d'Orchidiopsis, son anatomie, son développement. C. r. Soc. biol. Rh. *516;* 28.

BEILIG, W. (1954): Ein vanadiumhaltiger Eiweisssymplex aus den nasalen Fangfäden von Emunctator. S. H. Z. physiol. Chem. *884;* 55.

BITBRAIN, J. D. (1946): Anatomical and histological study of the nose of a Rhinogradent, Rhinolimacius. J. gen. Anat. *509;* 18.

———— (1950): The Rhinogradents. Univ. Press S. Andrews.

BLEEDKOOP, FR. (1945): Das Nasobemproblem. Z. v. Lit. *34;* 205.

BÖKER, H. (1935 and 1937): Einführung in die vergleichende Anatomie der Wirbeltiere. Fischer, Jena.

BOUFFON, L. (1953): A propos du système nutritif des Rhinogradents. Bull. Darwin Inst. Hi. *7;* Suppl. 2.

———— (1954): A propos du groupe polyphylétique des Rhinocolumnides. Bull. Darwin Inst. Hi. *8;* 12.

BOUFFON, L., and GAUKARI-SUDUR, O. (1952): L'anatomie comparée des Polyrrhines. Bull. Darwin Inst. Hi. *6;* 33.

BOUFFON, L., IRRI-EGINGARRI, J., and CHAIBLIN, FR. (1953): A propos de l'innervation du nasoire des Polyrrhines. C. r. Soc. Biol. Rh. *515;* 24.

BOUFFON, L., and LO-IBILATZE-SUDUR, Ch. (1954): Comment Orchidiopsis attire-t-elle sa proie? La nature (P) *77;* 311.

BOUFFON, L., and SCHPRIMARSCH, J. (1950): Concernant la question de la descendance du genus endémique Hypsiboas. Bull. Darwin Inst. Hi. *4;* 441.

BIBLIOGRAPHY

BOUFFON, L., and ZAPARTEGINGARRI, V. (1953): Sur l'embry-
ologie des Orchidiopsides. Bull. Darwin Inst. Hi. *7; 16.*

BROMEANTE DE BURLAS Y TONTERIAS, J. (1948): A systemática
dos Rhinogradentes. Bull. Darwin Inst. Hi. *2; 45.*

—— (1948a): Systematic studies on the new order of the
Rhinogradents. Am. Nat. F. *374; 1498.*

—— (1949): Os Polyrrhines e a derivaçâo d'elles. Boll. Braz.
Rhin. *1; 77.*

—— (1950): A derivaçâo e a árvore genealógica dos Rhinogradentes. Boll. Braz. Rhin. *2; 1203.*

—— (1951): The Rhinogradents. Bull. Darwin Inst. Hi. *5;*
Suppl.

—— (1952): The Hypogeonasidae. Bull. Darwin Inst. Hi. *6;*
120.

—— (1954): The hides of Rhinogradents and their grain.
Nature (Danuddlesborough) *92; 2.*

BROWN, A. B., and BITBRAIN, J. D. (1948): A simple electronically controlled substitute for feeding Mercatorrhinus. J.
psych. a. neur. contr. *181; 23.*

BUCHNER, P. (1953): Endosymbiose der Tiere mit pflanzlichen
Mikroorganismen. Birkhäuser, Basel.

COMBINATORE, M. (1943): Un pezzo di legno appuntato, trovato
sulla spiaggia di Owsuddowsa. Lav. preist. (Milano) *74; 19.*

D'EPP, Fr. (1944): La descendance des Polyrrhines. C. r. Soc.
biol. Rh. *506; 403.*

DEUTERICH, T. (1944): Ein hölzerner Suppenlöffel von Haida-
daifi. Z. f. v. Prähist. *22; 199.*

—— (1944a): Grundsätzliches über die Essbestecke der
Huacha-Hatschi, eines ausgestorbenen polynesisch-bajuwa-
rischen Mischvolkes. *ibid. 24; 312.*

FREDDURISTA, P., and PERISCHERZI, N. (1948): Il cambiamento
di colore fisiologico nei mammiferi, specialemente nei generi
Hexanthus e Cephalanthus (Polyrrhina, Rhinogradentia)
Arch. di fisiol. comp. ed. irr. *34; 222.*

BIBLIOGRAPHY

GAUKARI-SUDUR, O., BOUFFON, L., and PAIGNIOPOULOS, A. (1950): L'anatomie comparée des Sclérorrhines. C. r. Soc. Biol. Rh. *512;* 39.

GRUHLE, H. W. (1947): Ursache, Grund, Motiv, Auslösung. Festschr. f. KURT SCHNEIDER, Heidelberg, Scherer.

HARROKERRIA, J., and IRRI-EGINGARRI, J. (1949): Note sur la biologie d'Otopteryx volitans. C. r. Soc. Biol. Rh. *511;* 56.

HYDERITSCH, F. (1948): The slug which was a mammal. Sci.a. med. cinemat. Cie, Black Goats.

IZECHA, F. (1949): La primitividad de la cola de los Rhinogradentes. Boll. Arg. Rhin. *2;* 66.

JERKER, A. W., and CELIAZZINI, S. (1953): The ancestors of the Hypogeonasidae, were they Emunctators? Evolution (Littletown) *51;* 284.

JESTER, M. O., and ASSFUGL, S. P. (1949): The genus Dulcicauda and the problem of "Rassenkreis." Bull. Darwin Inst. Hi. *3;* 211.

LUDWIG, W. (1932): Das Rechts-Links-Problem im Tierreich und beim Menschen. Berlin.

——— (1954): Die Selektionstheorie. In: Die Evolution der Organismen. Hrsgeg. v. G. HEBERER. Fischer, Stuttgart.

MAYER-MEIER, R. (1949): Les "Triclades" de MUELLER-GIRMADINGEN, sont ils des mammifères? Bull. biol. mar. St. V. H. *17;* 1.

MORGENSTERN, CHR. (1905): Galgenlieder. B. Cassirer—Berlin.

MÜLLER-GIRMADINGEN, P. (1948): Les triclades des sables du Wisi-Wisi. Acta Helvetica Nas. Ser. B. *15;* 210.

NAQUEDAI, BR. B. (1948): Georrhinida et Hypogeonasida, deux subtribes parentés. C. r. Soc. biol. Rh. *510;* 64.

PETTERSSON-SKÄMTKVIST, E. (1943): The discovery of the Hi-Iay-Archipelago. J. A. geogr. *322;* 187.

——— (1946): Aventyrer på Haiaiai-öerna. Nyströms Förlag och Bokhandel, Lilleby.

PUSDIVA, FR. (1953): Über die Schleimdrüsen und die proteolytischen Prozesse in der Sellarscheibe von Dulcicauda griseaurella. S. H. Z. physiol. Chemie *822;* 1443.

REMANE, A. (1954): Die Geschichte der Tiere. In: Die Evolution der Organismen, hrsgeg. v. G. HEBERER. Fischer, Stuttgart.

RENSCH, B. (1947): Neuere Probleme der Abstammungslehre. Stuttgart.

SCHUTLIWITZKIJ, I. I. (1947): Hat Morgenstern die Rhinogradentier gekannt? (Russisch mit dtsch. Zusammenfassung.) Lit. prom. N. S. *27;* 81.

SHIRIN TAFARUJ (1954): A propos du chimisme du suc attractif des Nasolimacides. J. physiol. irr. *11;* 74.

SPASMAN, O., and STULTÉN, D. (1947): Rhinogradenternas systemet. Acta Scand. Rhin. *4;* 1.

SPUTALAVE, E. (1946): Le sabbie miliolidiche del orizzonte D 16 β superiore dell'isola Miruveely. G. geogr. fredd. Ital. *199;* 12.

STULTÉN, D. (1949): The descendency of the Polyrrhines. Bull. Darwin Inst. Hi. *3;* 31.

——— (1950): The anatomy of the nasarium of Hopsorrhinus. Bull. Darwin Inst. Hi. *4;* 511.

——— (1955): The evolution of turbellarians, a review of new aspects. Piltdown Univ. press.

STÜMPKE, H. (1956): Das Nasarium der Polyrrhinen, eine Zusammenfassung der bisherigen Ergebnisse, unter besonderer Berücksichtigung der neueren Untersuchungen über die Innervierung. Zool. Jahrb. Abt. XXXI, *43;* 497.

TASSINO DI CAMPOTASSI, I. (1955): Un "releaser" sopranormale in Mammontops. G. psicol. comp. e com. *2;* 714.

TRUFAGURA, A. (1948): La cola de los Rhinogradentes. Boll. Arg. Rhin. *1;* 1.